THE MASTER

RALPH POTTS

© Copyright 2005 Ralph Potts.
All rights reserved. No part of this publication may be reproduced, stored in a retrieval system, or transmitted, in any form or by any means, electronic, mechanical, photocopying, recording, or otherwise, without the written prior permission of the author.

Note for Librarians: A cataloguing record for this book is available from Library and Archives Canada at www.collectionscanada.ca/amicus/index-e.html
ISBN 1-4120-5558-X

TRAFFORD
PUBLISHING

Offices in Canada, USA, Ireland and UK
This book was published *on-demand* in cooperation with Trafford Publishing. On-demand publishing is a unique process and service of making a book available for retail sale to the public taking advantage of on-demand manufacturing and Internet marketing. On-demand publishing includes promotions, retail sales, manufacturing, order fulfilment, accounting and collecting royalties on behalf of the author.

Book sales for North America and international:
Trafford Publishing, 6E–2333 Government St.,
Victoria, BC v8t 4p4 CANADA
phone 250 383 6864 (toll-free 1 888 232 4444)
fax 250 383 6804; email to orders@trafford.com

Book sales in Europe:
Trafford Publishing (uk) Limited, 9 Park End Street, 2nd Floor
Oxford, UK ox1 1hh UNITED KINGDOM
phone 44 (0)1865 722 113 (local rate 0845 230 9601)
facsimile 44 (0)1865 722 868; info.uk@trafford.com

Order online at:
trafford.com/05-0456

10 9 8 7 6 5 4 3 2

FOREWORD

BEING THE SON OF my father has been a mixed blessing. He was away so often on voyages to distant corners of the world, or to the not so distant great ports of the Tyne and Merseyside, or London's Docklands that bustled in those days with working derricks and great cranes. He would return home with gifts other children could only dream of and a treasure trove of stories, some real, some imagined. Pedro, cast adrift and becalmed in a foggy Bay of Biscay, somehow gets mixed up in my mind with the chickens being shooed out of an operating theatre in the Caribbean, or the coconut shell being used to repair a badly fractured skull in the Indian Ocean. Somewhere, woven into it all are Belfast's terraced streets and dishcloth sky and the company of actors, great and tragic, that constituted its commercial life. Throughout the book are shards of black Belfast humour, like the glass strewn across the floor of his shipping company offices by an IRA Bomb concealed in a coffin.

My recollections of all these episodes are imperfect and unreliable now. So it seemed important to capture this trove of unique and enthralling tales, the sum of which are more than the life that lived them.

As the twentieth century recedes from our consciousness it becomes important too to remind us of the social realities of that era – when manufacturing and shipping defined the British economy and shaped our self-perception. The Second World War casts its long shadow over much of the book – from the German Blitz of Belfast City to the recent resurgence in acts of remembrance on key anniversaries – especially those relevant to seafarers.

The Master is written in a direct and vernacular style that captures the pugnacious spirit of the author. It is a compelling story of one man's battle against the vicissitudes of life. The pages are encrusted with sea salt and pitted with pearls of wisdom – read and be inspired, amused, angered and entertained.

David Potts
July 2005

A DEDICATION

The contents of this book are true in so far as my memory allows. It is also my wife's book; in as much as she was my sheet anchor as I travelled the world. Whilst she maintained the family home for our three children each of whom actively encouraged me to write this book.

TABLE OF CONTENTS

CHAPTER ONE 1
Visit to Belfast docks with mother
CHAPTER TWO 13
Return to Belfast after the German Blitz
CHAPTER THREE 22
Knocked down by tramcar
CHAPTER FOUR 34
Joined my first ship
CHAPTER FIVE. 54
Royal Mail Line "*Loch Gowan*"
CHAPTER SIX. 69
Trouble in the Yemen
CHAPTER SEVEN. 81
Canadian Pacific Steamships "*Empress of Canada*"
CHAPTER EIGHT. 86
Formed: International Shipping Services
CHAPTER NINE. 96
First ship taken on charter
CHAPTER TEN 107
I became a Member of the Baltic Exchange
CHAPTER ELEVEN 117
Turkey levies a surcharge on its roads

CHAPTER TWELVE 127
   Voluntary liquidation of "International Shipping Services"
CHAPTER THIRTEEN 140
   Returned to Seafaring
CHAPTER FOURTEEN 150
   Trip to South America in *"Washington"*
CHAPTER FIFTEEN 159
   Take command of *"Ashington"*
CHAPTER SIXTEEN.................... 175
   Trouble with the Inland Revenue
CHAPTER SEVENTEEN................ 180
   Land sick seaman in Milazzo
CHAPTER EIGHTEEN 198
   Attacked by thugs in Porto Veseme
CHAPTER NINETEEN................ 207
   Peace with the Inland Revenue
CHAPTER TWENTY 217
   Permanent command of *"Donnington"*
CHAPTER TWENTY ONE.............. 230
   Stowaway found onboard
CHAPTER TWENTY TWO.............. 243
   The storm of October 1987
CHAPTER TWENTY THREE............ 254
   Severe fog and ice in the Baltic
CHAPTER TWENTY FOUR 271
   Merchant Navy Association

CHAPTER ONE

I HELD MUM'S HAND very tight as we walked towards the edge of the quay in the Belfast docks. I was rather timorous going near the edge of the quay, mum said.

"I thought you would just love to see such a big ship. I read in the newspaper that she had come all the way from Australia with a full cargo of grain. We should see Norman he was coming to visit the docks with his friend Billy to day."

There she laid in all her glory her masts reaching for the sky the four masted barque *Moshulu*. The last of the great grain ships the date 18th. October 1938 when I had reached the stately age of five years old. There was Norman my brother eight years my senior waving and shouting to mum and I, he was so excited to be playing onboard such a magnificent ship. The months rolled by and mum took me to England for a holiday. Each day on holiday we watched men stretching barbed wire along the beaches. People were building funny looking tin huts in their garden eventually we headed home from Newcastle upon Tyne. We had been on holiday with mother's friends at Wallsend.

To a little boy the ship we were sailing on from Stranraer to Larne seemed like an ocean liner instead of the rather small local ferry the *Princess Margaret*. As I played on deck with my toy trolley bus mum seemed to be doing a lot of talking to one of the crew enquiring how my brother Norman might join the Merchant Navy. I had the distinct feeling he wasn't the captain. As he stood holding open the door of what seemed to be a cooking area judging by the smells emanating from the area, which might be the galley. The man holding the door was wearing a white tee shirt and blue small checked trousers. As the boat train pulled into the LMS Railway station at Belfast my sister Margaret accompanying Norman met us coming of the Larne boat train. It was dark outside as we left the station. Not having too far to walk as we lived near by we all walked up home together. Mum seemed to be greatly engrossed in conversation with Norman. It was Saturday night the 2nd September 1939.

My mother was obsessed with the church. Sunday morning was spent in church, Sunday afternoon in Sunday school, Sunday night again in church the whole family suffered religious indoctrination all day Sunday. This time I knew something was taking place. The sexton walked up the centre isle and whispered something in the minister's ear. The minister, to get the attention of the congregation held up his arms stating he had a most important announcement to make. I didn't understand all he said except something about the country was now at war with Germany after which there seemed an awful lot of praying.

The laughter seemed to have left the older people. The talk seemed to be about the different ones in the neighbourhood who had joined the army. Many men seemed to be with the Territorial Army across the water. At night it as just very dark all the busses and what cars that were about had their headlights covered with just a very tiny light showing. All the tramcar windows were covered with only a very tiny hole to look through to see your next stop.

I was told I was going away for a lovely holiday soon about May maybe when the nice weather arrived. Somehow when this holiday was mentioned the look on mums face seemed to convey another message. We lived with an old aunt, when I heard Margaret by sister say to her "Does he really have to go?" Old Joe at the corner says the Jerry planes couldn't fly this far. I saw Aunt Maggie signal to Margaret that I was listening to what was being said; I just knew something wasn't right about this so-called holiday.

Eventually the truth came out I was being evacuated to Ardglass in May for my own safety with all the other children in the district. It was a beautiful Sunday morning in May when all the children of the neighbourhood assembled in Mountcollyer School. Mothers were crying but the children were laughing, I wondered why. Each had their gas mask with them and a little case with a change of underwear and nightclothes. A rather large label was attached to our coats. After everyone had been checked and labelled we were taken out to buses, which were waiting to take us to the railway station, the Belfast and County Down Railway. At the railway station we were lined up at long tables manned by the Salvation Army and the Red Cross. Each evacuee was presented with a paper bag containing one ham sandwich an ice diamond and a dead flies grave (current square) plus a mug of scalding tea.

Eventually everyone boarded their respective trains whilst the grown ups cried the children laughed and pushed as one did on a Sunday school annual outing. After an hour or so the train pulled into Downpatrick where we detrained. Kindly ladies looked at our labels got us by the scruff of the neck and pushed us onto buses which delivered us much bewildered evacuees to the various towns and villages throughout the countryside. I debussed in the fishing village of Ardglass by the Presbyterian Church to be met by the family with whom I was to stay. Cecil and Janet Watts and their daughter Rosemary, Cecil was the local chemist.

They were cousins of mine some way or another a rather convoluted story of relationships in years past. Rosemary and I became good friends and remain so to this day. She was about eighteen months younger than I.

The view from their house was wonderful it was unobstructed right across the harbour and the Irish Sea. On a clear day it was possible to see the Isle of

Man and watch the fishing fleet put to sea and arrive home again from the fishing grounds. When I first sat at the table by the window. Janet glared at me and barked, "Get your elbows off the table."

The next rule was to learn how to shake Mrs Huskins hand and say "Good evening Mrs Huskins."

Or what ever the time of day was. Learn those two rules and one could do no wrong. Throughout my stay with the Watts family they were so kind and really endeavoured to do their very best for me. Though my mother arrived in Ardglass on the warpath once when she learned somehow that I had commenced attending the local Presbyterian Church. She demanded that arrangements were made forthwith for me to attend the local Church of Ireland Sunday school and church instead.

The local school was just one big room in which all the classes were held. The young kids faced the bottom of the class and the older children faced the front of the class. There was just one teacher Miss Addeson with a fearsome temper. I think the teacher's time was spent trying to control a room full of kids of all ages rather than teaching them. The summertime seemed to be spent largely in the playground.

Cecil seemed to be the honorary doctor to the fishing fleets. Much of his time was spent dressing cuts and bites from big jellyfish. They would come up to Cecil's chemist shop to obtain medical attention. Through their visits to the shop and Cecil's best endeavours I was able to arrange many trips to sea with the fishing fleet. My time spent in Ardglass seemed to be in, on and about the fishing boats especially the *Olive leaf* and the *Splendour.* The summer evenings saw the herring fleet put to sea many of which were Scottish boats, in the winter time the whiting fleet operated out of Ardglass.

On the night of the 7th. April 1941 Cecil awakened me as he opened the front door there was a considerable noise of aircraft droning overhead, which was unheard of in sleepy old Ardglass. Cecil told me to get something warm on which I did just as Janet arrived on the scene. He said come a long and we will go up to the castle, which was a military barrack at that time. Just as we opened the front gate the whole world lit up from the sky. Looking up wards I felt rather frightened but Cecil took my hand and we walked very quickly round the front of the town. The light in the sky became lower but as it did so it seemed to be on something like a parachute. From the hill on which the castle stood we could see flames in the distance and hear explosives many men stood about and by the tone of their voices seemed somewhat afraid if not very scared. One man said, *"*I think Belfast is getting it".

"Getting what," I said.

At that Cecil, said "Lets get home*"*

As he put his arm round my shoulders I had a feeling that he was very apprehensive about something.

On Easter Tuesday at 10:45 I was lying awake talking to Cecil who was sitting on the edge of my bed when what started as the noise of aircraft in the distance became deafening as they came closer. I went to the window and quickly got dressed, as did the whole of Ardglass everyone congregated at the seafront. I followed Cecil again up the hill to the castle this time the whole town was lit up by flares. In the distance the sky was red and changing colour with flashes, the noise was frightening everyone was so excited and very frightened. Many people had beads in their hands, which I had never seen before. As usual Cecil tried to explain what they were, prayer beads which Roman Catholic people used to help them with their prayers. He suggested that I should ask my wee friend Desmond to explain to me all about the beads. We headed home smartly. Janet had stayed with Rosemary who was still in bed fast asleep. Janet and Cecil decided between them if Janet could get through to Belfast she would try and get the train at breakfast time. She decided to take me with her to make sure my mother and the family were ok and to convince me I had nothing to worry about for their sake.

As it happened we had to wait until later in the week because of the numbers of people leaving the city, travelling would have been impossible my train. In the meantime my uncle and aunt together with my cousin Doreen arrived from Belfast by car and were able to tell us all the news about the family. Mum apparently was a bit of a hero she continually ran in and out our house and the air raid shelter making tea for everyone helping, to keep their sprits up. Here in Ardglass the Fisherman's Rest by the harbour was filled with evacuees from Belfast trying to find accommodation in the town and surrounding district.

All education more or less ceased. With the influx of evacuees the wee school just could not cope with the numbers. Eventually another teacher arrived a male. The older children the more senior classes faced one way towards the front of the one classroom and the junior classes the other way but that still left the room with what seemed to be a constant hum of noise. The teachers couldn't keep control although there wasn't any real disruption nevertheless one paid little attention really to what was going on around them. Once the sun shone classes were as far as possible taken in the playground. My time was spent climbing about fishing boats with the bulk of my schoolwork being done for me by a very good young friend who also made his career in the Merchant Navy.

On the 4th.May I was taken to Belfast to visit my family who were staying with other relatives Uncle Charlie and Aunt Ruth out at Niells Hill. That night the sky seemed to be filled with searchlights darting about. It wasn't long until the sirens went off when we all followed uncle Charlie down to the shooting range at the back of the house. The shooting range was a wonderful place to shelter from the bombing and machine-gunning from the German gunners in the planes. It was a Sunday night and most people didn't really know what was going on but I think they all expected to meet the German army in the street. Everyone was bewildered. When we arrived home to aunt Ruth's house it was decided that perhaps we should stay a little longer together seeing as the family were together and just wait and see what happens. We did stay a few days but I gather mother was rather anxious to get me back to Ardglass. The day after we arrived back there was a terrible commotion on the beach all the children that had been playing in the water came running out of the water screaming. I went into the water to see what had frightened them. There was what seemed to be a large collection of sea weed, paper and rubbish all sticking together floating near the waters edge.

On closer inspection I was sure it was a dead body. I commenced to push the body into shallower water and when it grounded on the sandy bottom I and another youngster pulled it up the beach a little further best we could. It was a dead body the other kids by this time had created such a commotion that people arrived from everywhere including the police. Two men from the harbour office arrived with a stretcher and with the help of the police took the body round to the harbour office. Speculation was rife, everyone was sure it was a shot down German airman even though the body seemed to have little clothes on it. I think Cecil being the local chemist and honorary local doctor he too was called to the harbour office. The rule was in the district no matter what happened 'get Cecil' he was highly respected by everyone to the extent that some people thought Christ was only a tenderfoot compared to him. Rumour was such that everyone was convinced there had been many German aircraft shot down and that the crews were hiding in the countryside. There was many soldiers and police searching everywhere for downed airmen but it was all in peoples imagination. Seven guns and a catapult only, defended Belfast, in fact there was no planes shot down over the city.

In September I was trying to catch crabs in a rock pool when a voice called out, "Hello Ralph what are you doing."

There was my brother Norman standing on the rocks holding a lovely blue coloured model yacht. When I looked closer at the yacht I knew it was Norman's own yacht.

"What are you doing with that yacht down here?" I asked.

He handed me the yacht and said "It's for you I won't need it anymore. I'm going into the Merchant Navy in a few days."

At that I put it into the water. The wind caught it and away it went at quite a rate of knots across the harbour. Norman ran round to the harbour and then down the harbour wall and retrieved the yacht before it might have passed the wall and out to sea. That would have been it away for good.

I was excited for him going away to sea but at the same time sad because as brothers we were quite close. I suppose really we hadn't much option as kids but to be close. My father had died when I was about seven months old and mum had to go out to work. He had been wounded twice in France during the 1914-18 war whilst serving with the Canadian army. After he came out of the military hospital he never really worked again and was discharged from the army. Although Norman was eight years older than I he was left with the job as the proverbial baby sitter. Once when there just was no one for me to stay with after lunch, Norman was left with no option but to take me back to school with him. I spent the afternoon in the big boys class complete in my leather-buttoned gaiters.

It was late October when my mother had come to visit me in Ardglass. Just after tea when the evenings the were getting dark. It was one of those misty nights when the streetlights seemed to have a halo round them. Mother and Janet were having a row what it was all about I don't know. Mother set off for the railway station with the tears running down her face. Both Janet and Cecil forbade me to go after her. Eventually I broke away from their hold on me and ran after my mother. I couldn't see where I was running; my tears were restricting my eyesight. At the station mum was standing alone, she seemed quite distressed at that point Cecil arrived at the station also. When he ordered me to come home I just refused and created quite a rumpus in order to get going home to Belfast with my mother. The train was sitting in the station. After mum had words with Cecil over something or other she boarded the train instructing me to get onboard the train also. I wasn't wearing a coat just a jersey when I run after mum from Cecil's house. Anyway mum put her coat around me and held her close to her to keep me warm as we rattled our way to Belfast in the old boneshaker of a train. To this day I have no idea what the row was all about. I am quite sure it had nothing to do regarding my treatment during my stay in Ardglass with my cousins. As a wee boy everyone was always very kind to me. It was always very difficult for mother, trying to provide for us three children as a widow. Naturally from time to time she was hard but we didn't do to badly really. She did her very best for us at all times under the circumstance.

CHAPTER TWO

On arrival at the railway station in Belfast it was very dark. The blackout was in operation there were no streetlights and all lights on vehicles were covered with just a little slit to let a little light through. We got onboard a darkened tramcar for Whitla Street, which was only a short walk from where we lived. At least I thought that was were we lived. Whilst living in Ardglass our old home had been damaged during the blitz in fact the whole area had been destroyed. The only building left standing was our church, Saint Paul, Church of Ireland. The family had moved to a new home in a new area, which was really only two tram stops away. It was near to playing parks, and was really very good.

It was decided by my mother and aunt that the sooner I commenced school the better for everyone by that it was meant there would be someone to keep and eye on me whilst everyone was at work. That is my sister who worked in what was deemed to be the oldest newspaper office in the world the Northern Wig. Having been a nurse in France during the First World War, Aunt Maggie that is the proverbial Aunt Maggie helped Mann a First Aid Post in Belfast.

I was given strict instructions to always watch the barrage balloons of which there was one stationed beside our home If they went up very high into the sky I was to run to old friends and neighbours from our previous home who lived about a mile away. I must not wait for the air raid sirens to sound. Very often when the balloons went up, I would run like hell, even though no sirens sounded. The airmen who manned the station were just keeping the winding apparatus in good working order. Soon I ignored my instructions and only run to our old neighbours if the sirens sounded. Should the sirens sound after we had gone to bed the drill was to get up quickly get dressed and proceed to the air raid shelter. If the sirens sounded at night we didn't have to go to school the next day.

I had got so far behind with my schoolwork for various reasons mostly the fact that I did no work. There wasn't anyone at home to make me work. Soon schooling was to become a very big problem. It was more exciting and very much more interesting to slip unseen into the docks and climb over military equipment especially American Lightings and Thunderbolts fighters, tanks and generally make a nuisance of ones self. On the dock gates there were American Naval and Military Police together with British Military and Naval Police but they never seemed to see a couple of wee boys slipping into the docks between the dock gate and the train which operated between the docks the railway and the general goods yard. It was all a very exciting time for a youngster. Often it was possible to get up the gangway of the old First World War cruiser HMS Caroline. The Caroline was part of the DEMS (Defence Equipped Merchant Ship) organisation and therefore full of aircraft recognition posters and lots of interesting booklets. The idea was to distract the guard on the gangway by having a couple of kids appear to be interfering with the moorings. The mission was to get onboard and get the hold of aircraft recognition posters. They could be sold to other kids for at least a penny if not three. Should the guard manage to hit you with his stick you would remember it for many weeks afterwards. Once I had settled at school the routine was as usual except when the air-raid sirens sounded. In one of our classes, Albert one of the pupils always fainted when the sirens sounded. It was the air-raid precaution rule to stand at ones desk and when instructed march in an orderly manner to the air raid shelter. Our habit was to stand at our desks, watch for Albert to faint and once he fainted march out to the air raid shelter.

It was a rule my mother had to encourage me at school. If I were progressing at school mother would buy me a flower. Usually a single tulip in a little red flower bowel. Unfortunately I once lied to my mother, I had not progressed as she thought I had. She had been to see my teacher who was a very close friend of hers and learned my brains were crushed every time I walked. I was out in the back when I heard my mother enter the house and shout at the top of her voice.

"Boy, come hear boy." Seldom did she ever use such a tone in her voice. When I saw her she had that vinegar look about her face. She hit me and I fell against the yard wall, next the flowerpot she had bought came flying through the air. As I lay on the ground it landed on my head. What a sight that must have been, me on the ground against the wall with a tulip appearing to come from my head.

What did come out of the flying flowerpot episode was the realisation that something had to be done regarding schooling. I needed to work to make up for my years at the little country school in Ardglass. My attitude to learning with respect to schooling in general had to change. Mother solved the problem by making it quite clear to me that if I wanted to go to sea like Norman I would have to excel at school. To make up for wasted time I would have to go to school at night, but I was too young for that. Problem solved you will go on Saturday afternoons. That in fact was what I did. Some guy had opened his home to youngsters who needed extra lessons. He took the classes himself and was really quite good. The lessons seemed to be more enjoyable than at ordinary school. It transpired that there were many children who needed a little boost with their education due largely to the general disruption of their education. Being bombed out of their homes. Evacuated to the country, mothers working who had never gone out to work before all added to the general confusion and uncertainty.

Extra schooling was one thing but when mother deemed it imperative that I learn more about my church I felt like stowing away on a ship. Maybe Norman would help me. I was made attend extra Sunday school classes, which meant enrolling in what was known as the diocesan medal class. This meant on a Sunday afternoon one went from Sunday school to the diocesan medal class instead of home like the other kids. It also required attending a class on a Thursday night. The biggest shock to me was, I really enjoyed the classes. The contents of the class lessons were the history of Ireland and its church rather than Bible studying.

The first American troops of the 34th.Division arrived at the Dufferan Dock onboard the British Liner *Strathaird*. That was quite an exciting day for everyone. The Americans whilst billeted throughout the Province a large contingent was based at the top of our avenue in the Grove Park. Our milkman delivered milk to the American army camp. When he let us help him it entailed carrying crates of milk to the back door of the army cook house. All the cooks appeared to be coloured soldiers with big smiles on their faces. They seemed to take great delight in giving us kids very large pieces of chocolate cake and ice cream. If one was lucky you might also get some packets of chewing gum. It soon became a sort of game though not I might say for the American service men. If one saw a Yank, as they were affectionately known, with a girl especially near any secluded place they would be sure to give you sixpence if not a shilling to go away and give them peace. Some chewing gum was always a prerequisite.

Whilst playing with a gang of kids up by Hazelbank what is now the zoological gardens. I and another boy 'Sleepy' Hampton my very good friend was hiding in a tree from the others. In the meantime a Yank came along not knowing we were in the tree of course. He and his lady friend sat at the bottom of the tree. He slipped his arm around the girl and then opened her dress. We could hear her moaning a little and when we moved along our branch to see what was wrong with her, we lost our balance and came tumbling out of the tree right on top of the Yank and the girl. We were quickly on our feet and away; I don't think we stopped running until we arrived home. I think I can still hear the yells of the couple in my ears to this day.

By early 1944 it seemed all the Americans had left Northern Ireland. This was in preparation of the invasion of North Africa. I had come into school one morning in the midst of great excitement it was the 6th. June 1944 I think everyone was talking about the landings at Normandy. In celebration we were allowed home early from school. When I ran home and into the house so excited to tell mum what had happened, she already new. Mother had been out and bought every newspaper she could. The house was full of papers. On our walls in the kitchen we had two large maps, one of the North African fronts and one of the Russian front. With little flags on them which we moved in accordance with the troops advance on the battlefronts. Nothing would do mum but that she would get down to the newsagents to try and obtain a map of the Normandy front but she was rather soon to obtain maps of the Normandy front.

A couple of days before the Normandy landings we had had a letter from Norman which was postmarked Montevideo, Uruguay, Mum was very happy knowing Norman was well away from Normandy. That afternoon we had gone out to the shops were we met a lady from our church. I didn't know her name but mum knew her very well. Poor woman she was in an awful state her son was serving with one of the regiments, which was known to have been among the first assault troops. Later in the year Norman eventually arrived home for some leave loaded with the usual presents. Usually a nice belt for me, I had a penchant for nice belts. His next ship was engaged in carrying prisoners of war from the continent to England.

He sent me endless German badges and on one occasion brought home a German helmet for me. As I got older and ceased to play with such things it ended up a very useful flowerpot.

After the flying bomb sites were overrun by the Allied troops people began to feel more relieved. It was always felt that the bombs might reach Belfast and we would all be evacuated again. When the European war ended in May 1945 and then the Japanese war ended in August 1945 everyone felt so happy and relieved that we children just lived for the day that everything would return to normal as promised by our parents. I suppose really the mood of the people was infectious. Everyone looked to the day when the soldiers would come home.

The Burma boys had been away four years. The whole city went to the LMS station to welcome them home. That day Field Marshal Montgomery arrived at the City Hall and a great many people went to the City Hall to welcome him.

Unfortunately it wasn't joyous for all the troops there were those who came home to wives and girlfriends who had found other men friends whilst their husbands and boyfriends served overseas and so the gossipmongers had a real field day. Some homes were really sad places to visit. The children from the homes in which there was wartime domestic strife just did not want to acknowledge their pals in any shape or form, they had became very withdrawn

The docks were full of ships many of which especially the corvettes and armed trawlers were being converted to peacetime use. Troopships were bringing troops home and taking troops away. The Belgian troops were all returning home. Some ships arrived home with Prisoners of War who had been released. The docks were even more fascinating than ever they had been there was just so much activity. Especially when the GI brides were leaving there were crowds on the quayside to see the American war brides go of to meet their new husbands in America.

On a beautiful summer evening 1946 two youngsters including myself went into the docks to make our usual boyish raid on the HMS Caroline. Unfortunately the gangway guard caught us. Whilst holding me by the ear, which was very painful I might say, an officer appeared who sent for the police typical English keep to the rules. The police arrived, a harbour constable on a big pushbike asked us what were we doing here as if he didn't know. He had caught us before many times over the years. We said in a rather proud manner "We had come to join the Sea Cadets".

At that he marched us up to just where, the sea cadets were forming up in drill order. He said to the drill officer "These boys have come to join you"

At that the drill officer shouted at us. "Get in line with those boys there."

The cadets were lined up in three columns. We ran over to the columns and took up our positions like old hands. Obviously we had to stay the remainder of the evening with the cadets otherwise we would have been in severe trouble. It so happened we enjoyed the evening so much that we returned the next drill evening and continued to do so for the next three years.

CHAPTER THREE

Enrolment for night classes was taking place being the first week in September. The classes were run by the Belfast College of Technology. I think the classes I enrolled in were pre-apprenticeship classes. My attendance at night classes and Saturday classes began to pay dividends because I became more confident with maths. I think this began to show in my schoolwork. As usual mother tried to push me scholastically. All grammar school education had to be paid for in those days there was no such thing as free education. An attempt was made to enrol me in the Belfast High School but because of my lack of a good scholastic record I was only accepted in the Preparatory School of the Belfast High. If I did well in the preparatory school I could sit the entrance examination for the High School proper next year and if successful enrol in the upper school. I felt all the time I was going backwards as enrolling in the preparatory school was backward step in my view. Somehow the money was scrapped together for the school fee.

I was thirteen years of age and everyone else in the class was eleven a couple of the boys and girls were twelve who like myself were trying to prove themselves worthy of acceptance into the upper school. I felt that I copped quite well with the work with the exception of languages. I was good at history and always top of the class in geography and not bad at art.

Although I was good at maths I had a phobia about them. One thing I will always be grateful to the High School for was my introduction to the world of classical music. Throughout my life music has given me many hours of pleasure.

Although I was not supposed to know anything about the struggle in the family to pay my school fees I knew all about it. Much to the annoyance of the school I did not take part in games, as there was no money for sports gear whatsoever. Nothing was said to me directly by my mother or anyone else but I did feel most strongly that I was becoming somewhat of a financial burden on the family. I rather think the family did not realize how much I knew and understood about the financial situation the family seemed to be in. I suppose I was considered to be too young to know anything about such matters as family finance.

Whilst travelling to school one morning on my bicycle I was knocked down by an old tramcar, one of the old boneshaker type, which had no drivers cab as such. The driver leaned over the front of the drivers driving position. Bawling and shouting at me as he pushed his goggles up over his eyes instead of giving a young boy some help in an accident. The drivers of those tramcars wore a large raincoat during inclement weather and also driver's goggles. As they did not have a protective cab. He might as well have killed me for what did happen. My school blazer was destroyed and I knew there just wasn't money for another one. I did have a note to take to school but it was really rough being "schooner rigged" compared to the other children. At times really rough because I had to wear an old ARP battle jacket, which is beyond description. It was the same as the soldiers wore during the Second World War except it was black in colour.

By this time my sister Margaret had taken a job in London. Her firm offered her a better job in the London office. The Merchant Navy still had the services of Norman, which he seemed to enjoy, making me green with envy. Every time he came home it was wonderful always presents and plenty of money for all the things a young lad loved. Unfortunately mum took a stroke. I found it very hard to cope as I had to litterly run the house including toileting my mother. One Sunday night mother took very ill, I called a doctor but she was beyond my ability to nurse or help her. I pleaded with the doctor as I cried my eyes out to take her away to hospital. I was at the top of the stairs, which had no light, standing holding a candle as I pleaded with him to take her. I assured him I would be all right to be left alone. I looked after myself for a few days until I too took ill with Giant Urticaria and the neighbours called a doctor. A couple of the neighbours attended me whilst I lay in bed. The doctor called in the morning and evening to give me injections. Eventually someone sent word to Margaret to tell her I was ill and mother was in hospital. A few days later Margaret arrived home from London mum came home from hospital. Mother was no sooner home from hospital than Margaret took off to London again and I became cook, slush and butler and school boy in body but certainly not in spirit once again.

I returned to school complete with black battle jacket. The geography teacher and I seemed to have great respect for each other notwithstanding a very unfortunate instant in class one afternoon. The geography teacher had an awful temper she carried in class a stick, which was short and thick which she had no hesitation about using on a pupil. On the afternoon in question she was giving the wee girl in the desk in front of me a very hard time. She then hit Betty with her pointer. I sprang at the teacher wrestled with her and took the geography pointer from her. The atmosphere in the class was electric. The students all seemed to be very frightened, young Betty was in tears. I suddenly had the feeling of what it must have been like to rob a bank. When one would be alone in the bank holding everyone at bay. The headmaster Dr Harte arrived on the scene and quietly asked me to accompany him to his office. In a very quiet voice he asked me to tell him what happened which I did in no uncertain manner. As it was approaching the end of the school day he suggested that I go on home quietly. I did so and assumed that was the end of the matter.

Some days later my mother received a letter asking her to attend the school. Mum was very ill, as she had really fallen into bad health. Norman was on leave so he went to see the headmaster. It was suggested that as I would be fourteen years of age on my next birthday the age at which a child could leave school in those days. The headmaster felt I was not fitting into the school in the way he would have wished. Furthermore it was well known in the school that it was my ambition to go to sea. It was suggested therefore that I should leave the school when I reached my fourteenth birthday. In the meantime he Dr. Harte would endeavour to get me into a nautical college somewhere. I knew if I did pass an entrance examination to any of the nautical colleges in England there would be absolutely no hope of the money needed to send me there to be forthcoming. True to his word the headmaster arranged for me to sit the entrance examination to HMS Worcester and Pangbourne, which together with HMS Conway were the three main Merchant Navy public schools for officer cadets. Knowing the financial situation at home it governed my attitude towards the examination. I approached the examination with an element of indifference, which was reflected in the results, I failed both examinations.

The months seemed to fly past and then it was my birthday the dizzy heights of fourteen years of age had been reached. The school broke up for the Christmas holidays; I left and signed on at the Local

Labour Exchange to find work. I got a job immediately at twelve shillings and sixpence per week (62.5 pence) with a linen firm pushing a wheel borrows around Belfast. They hadn't taken delivery of the wheel borrow yet. I was called into a director's office and told all about the wheelbarrow. It had four wheels not just two, which were pneumatic, the manner in which he described his wheelbarrow I thought sure he had mistaken it for a Rolls Royce.

The borrow was loaded with large bolts of linen which required delivering to various firm about the city of Belfast. Really it was an awful job and too heavy for me. It was more suitable for someone like Charles Atlas. The Donegal Road in Belfast has a small incline at the lower part of the road. One delivery I was required to make was up this incline. I tried to push the borrow up the hill, I couldn't, I tried pulling it up, I couldn't. I remembered how one whilst trying to ride a bicycle up a steep incline it was easier to attack an incline by riding up a hill at an angle. I tried that and couldn't move the thing. On the other side of the road was a telephone box and luckily I had two pennies in my pocket the cost of a phone call. I walked over to the box and telephoned the owners of the dam wheel borrow and told them were they could collect it. That was me finished with wheel borrows.

I soon had another job as a taper boy at fifteen shillings (75 pence) per week in Harland & Wolff. This job was interesting; it entailed taping armature windings for electric motors of all shapes and sizes. As a boy in the Electrical Manufacturing Shop it very often entailed being sent to help the men in a host of various and interesting tasks. It also very often required accompanying the finished unit out to the ships in the fitting out berths. At that period in the life of Harland & Wolff 1948 there were numerous vessels being built and many more being converted from troopships back to regular passenger work.

The building and engineering of ships was not really my forte. I wanted to be a navigating officer and someday command a ship. I was still serving in the Sea Cadets and doing very well. The previous year we had been taken to the Clyde onboard the 'HMS Attacker' to take part in the review of the fleet by King George VI. After the review we travelled from Gourock to Fareham via Portsmouth by train and spent two weeks onboard HMS Collingwood which was not a ship but what the Royal Navy called a stone frigate. It was a barracks and the main electrical school for the Royal Navy. Whilst at HMS Collingwood I had an accident with a young girl and ended up in the sick bay of the 'Collingwood' whilst in the sick bay as the sick bay attendant bandaged my leg he asked me if it was my intention to join the Royal Navy. I rather proudly for some reason or other said "No The Merchant Navy"

He said to me, which I thought rather strange "You're a very wise young man".

On arrival back in Belfast I was more determined than ever to get into the Merchant Navy. I felt I had pulled myself up educationally that I could cope with any entrance examinations necessary. Later in the year a new private pre-sea training college opened in Belfast by a Captain Skillen who promised to have cadets placed with shipping companies. The fees were modest compared to those charged by English colleges. It was soon to be known throughout the Province as Paddy Skillens sea factory. My brother came ashore and took a job as an instructor at the college. He was also directly responsible for obtaining appointments to shipping companies for many of the boys. Of the boys who passed through the college and who made a full career of the Merchant Navy, many eventually rose to command. A few of them rose to positions of influence within the industry especially the oil industry.

I enrolled in the college and thought I was on top of the world. Within weeks I had been accepted into the Anglo American Oil Company as an officer cadet on the strength of my school reports, reports from the Sea Cadets and my college reports. There was no entrance examination. Another cadet and I had to report to the Shipping Federation and the Mercantile Marine Office on the 15th.December 1949. We were documented; given a Merchant Navy Identity Card a Merchant Navy Discharge Book that would become a record of all the ships one would serve in and a seaman's ration slip. We would join the same ship in a week's time the oil tanker *Robert F Hand*. Bound for the West Indies. We would be paid a salary of £6. 5 shillings. Per month with immediate effect. I was in the Merchant Navy on full pay as an officer cadet and I just thought I was on top of the world. A few days later we both had a change of orders. We could have Christmas at home and join the oil tanker "*Esso London* on Humberside in the New Year bound for the Persian Gulf further instructions and travel tickets would arrive at our homes first week in January.

The week before leaving home my future shipmate Stephen threw a going away party in his house, which was wonderful. He had lots of beautiful young girls at the party but no alcohol drink. It wasn't expected at house parties for young people in those days. The night we went down to get the ferry over to Liverpool my brother Norman left me down to the ferry and helped me get my gear onboard. As I moved to the gangway of the ferry with Stephen a tide of humanity moved behind him. All his relations came down to the Liverpool boat to see him off. When she sailed we stayed up on deck to watch Belfast slowly slip further away astern as we steamed down the Lough. I think we were too excited to go to our cabin and get some sleep. We had been advised it would be a long slow train journey from Liverpool to Hull were we were booked into the Royal Station Hotel to await the ship berthing at Immingham.

A couple of days later the ships agent arrived at the hotel by car to take us to our first ship. There we were dressed up in our uniforms not really knowing what to expect. The agent seemed to be a very knowledgeable gentleman. He continued to tell us how wise we were joining the Merchant Navy as young cadets. I spotted the ship with a big Esso on the funnel and asked the agent at the same time trying to subdue the excitement in my voice. "Is that her, she's a big ship"

Anyway we struggled up the gangway with all our sea-going gear, the agent was able to show us to our cabin. This looks great, just lovely two bunks a settee a writing desk and a private bathroom and curtains on the portholes. This is better than my own home. The two of us went along to the Chief Officers cabin knocked on the cabin door respectfully a voice called out *"*Come in boys*"*

I stepped into his cabin and said. "Cadet Ralph Potts reporting sir".

Stephen my colleague did likewise. What a shock he then gave us. He looked us up and down and then said "I'm not going to take you to the captain to sign on, I'm going to wait until tomorrow. I want you to think about what your doing. Your fine young lads and quite mad going to sea*"*. He then proceeded to tell us just how terrible live at sea really is, suggesting we should put our education to much greater use.

Next morning we were awakened by a loud knock on our cabin door together with someone shouting, "Wakey, wakey, rise and shine do your bit for the Esso tanker line."

The voice of our illustrious 3rd Officer. He took us to the officer's saloon for breakfast, which was served to us by the officer's steward. A breakfast far in excess of anything we would have received at home. A choice of fruit juice together with a choice of cereal I asked for bacon and eggs says the steward "How many eggs"

I thought he was joking, that was rounded off by rice cakes and syrup, toast tea or coffee. After breakfast we reported to the chief officers office and told him we still wanted to go to sea whereupon he took us to the captain to sign on the ship. Having signed on he commenced giving us a lecture on behaviour and what was expected of us as officer cadets.

We were called at 0600 for a 0700 turn to at which time we would scrub the wheelhouse and chartroom, polish all the brass and if necessary hose down the bridge and captains deck. The cleanliness and maintenance of the bridge and captains deck was our responsibility. In the evening we would spend one hour on the bridge with the chief officer from 1800 until 1900 for instruction. From 2000 until 2100 we would spend with the 3rd officer practising signalling. Before arrival in the Red Sea we were expected to be very efficient with an aldis lamp and remain so throughout the voyage. The cadet's onboard Esso London would carry out in future all visual signalling onboard. The mate produced a coca tin with a small hole in it through which shown a small bulb connected to a battery the whole lot was then connected to an old morse key. If, and only if, we were considered worth it two afternoons per week free time would be given as study time. Saturday afternoon was devoted to cleanliness that was dobhing (doing your washing) and preparing ones cabin for the captain's inspection on a Sunday morning.

In port whilst working cargo a cadet would understudy an officer which really meant working six hours off and six hours on continuously. Very often the officers worked all the hours God sent them that meant we also worked such hours. The greatest workload was when trying to gas free the ship in preparation for loading at the loading port. During the first year of our cadetship we would work with the crew under the bos'un orders but under no circumstances were we allowed to familiarize with the crew. This proved to be a most difficult rule to abide bye as we worked all day with the lads, especially with the deck boys who were our own age.

CHAPTER FOUR

Soon we experienced the same knocking at our door and loud voice shouting "Stations, stations come on now all hands to stations." It was 0200 and the ship was preparing for sea the pilot was expected onboard in thirty minutes. The day you worked so hard for as a wee boy running to night school the Sea Cadets and nautical college. The chief officer suggested

That as this was our first trip we should just go to the bridge and watch what goes on. We could make tea for everyone on the bridge. On the bridge the 3rd. Officer explained the chart of the Humber to us, the tides were very strong for us sailing. We would come off the berth in a strong flood tide, a spring tide because the moon and the sun were in conjunction. The 3rd. officer explained this all to us as we waited for the pilot and captain to come onto the bridge. It was all becoming very interesting and exciting already.

The captain turned to the 3rd. officer and said single up fore & aft, the third officer passed the captains orders to the fore part and the after part of the ship. Soon the word came back to the bridge. Singled up fore & aft sir. The pilot soon gave the order 'let go forward hold on to the after back spring let everything else go aft.' I could see from the bridge the bow was swinging fast of the quayside. Let go aft, slow ahead, the pilot ordered, the after docking phone on the bridge rang. The third officer repeated the order quickly. The station aft called back very quickly 'clear aft' half ahead the pilot called to the third officer. Orders were being given fast and furious the third officer rang 'Half Ahead' on the engine room telegraph. I looked and smiled at Stephen whispering "We're away now Stephen"

We soon left Spurn Head lighthouse to port as the pilot cutter came alongside and our pilot disembarked. At the Humber light vessel the captain gave an order, which put us on a southerly course. He then turned to us both and said "You can turn in lads if the officers don't want you, six o'clock comes quickly."

Looking at the bridge clock I could see it is well past four already, does he really mean we still have to get up for a 7 o'clock turn too?

After breakfast we reported to the bos'un whom I had a bad feeling about. I had the feeling that he was one of these bosuns who liked to bully future officers. Unfortunately my feelings proved to be too true but one could learn a lot from him. The job in hand was to get the ship gas free as soon as possible this entailed rigging wind chutes into the cargo tanks. These were large circular canvas tubes with wind vanes at the top, which scooped up the wind forcing it into the tank expelling the gas, which is a dangerous residue from the cargo. It was imperative to gas free, tanks cleaned and clean ballast taken onboard before transiting the Suez Canal. In nine days time we should be at Port Said the entrance to the Suez Canal and in four days we should pass through the Straits of Gibraltar when either Stephen or I should be proficient enough to converse with Lloyds signal station by signal lamp. I was glad I had learned my signalling both with the Sea Cadets and the Nautical College in Belfast. I only needed to practise plenty over the next few days.

The wind freshened more and the sea became rather rough causing the ship to jump about a little, enough to make Stephen very sick. The chief officer sent him below but warned him the best thing to do if he can is to spend as much time in the open air as possible. The smell of a ship is unique a mixture of fuel oil and food cooking. The midship accommodation on a tanker is usually clear of such smells but it still has a funny smell if one could describe it as such. Stephen was soon back on his feet again in the good fresh air of the Bay of Biscay coping with the large swell on the beam experienced in the Bay. The chief steward who was also a sort of head nurse under the chief officer and the captain advised us cadets to be very careful about removing our shirts in the sun. It was suggested that we should remove our shirts for only a half hour on the first day in the heat and perhaps a full hour on the second day extending the period without a shirt each day by about half an hour.

We entered the Straits at night and were called up by the big Lloyds signal lamp. It flashed out "*What ship were from were bound*"?

I was on our lamp and replied 'Esso London Humber to Ras Tanura'

He then came back "*Bon Voyage*"

The third officer ordered me to give him a long flash a sort of courtesy flash.

Before arrival in the Straits the chief officer had carried out a gas test on all the tanks to see if it was safe to enter them. When the cargo is being discharged all the loose scale and rust on the side of the tanks falls into the tanks and must be removed before loading the next cargo. Physically having the crew enter the tanks and shovelling the scale and muck into buckets hauling it up out of the tank and throwing it overboard do this. It is a filthy laborious task. The crew put on their oldest clothes or as we did on the advise of the bos'un. Got an old flag, stripped naked and put the flag on like a baby's nappy. It can then be dumped overboard on completion of tank cleaning. At the end of the day everyone lined up at the chief officers office to receive their mandatory large tot of good navy rum to clear your innards. This was something again, real rum. Gosh! If my mother could just see me now. Three sheets to the wind and eyes like golf balls. Jezz! This Merchant Navy really is something.

On the ninth day we arrived into Port Said to

join the first southbound convoy. Convoys govern the traffic in the Canal. Each day two convoys transit the canal southwards and one transits northwards. The first southbound convoy ties up at the 'Farouk Cut' to allow the northbound convoy a passage north. My first foreign port was Port Said it was fascinating and a total hive of activity. A huge searchlight which acts as headlamp is connected up fo'ard, it has two beams lighting up both banks of the canal. Although a passage may be scheduled for daylight any delay will surely cause part of the passage to be in darkness, passage time being fourteen hours. The ubiquitous George Roby's bumboats with their numerous cheap wares came alongside immediately. Shirts for thirty shillings under- wear full set twenty shillings and endless wooden bookends all made from the same wooden cross on Calvary. The good Lord must have had some cross. The beauty of shopping on one of George Ruby's bumboats was one could sign for your purchases and the captain would deduct the sale from your wages. I'm sure in turn George looked after the old man. Two little rowing boats one on each side of the ship with a crew of two old men were also shipped. These two old boys would by using their rowing boats pull the mooring ropes to the canal bank in order to assist with tying up at the 'Farouk Cut'. Soon the convoy moved off down the canal where we saw the locals working near their little mud huts and beasts of burden. Often we observed a family consisting of usually an old boy sitting on the back of a poor old donkey as the wife walked along behind bowed down with what appeared to be cooking utensils. It was the local children who were forever trying to get onboard our ship when tied up in Port Said they could speak not only fluent English but in various UK dialects. They would mimic a Scots accent and shout, "My name is McGregor I'm from Glasgow where you from mate?"

At the Farouk Cut whilst tied up for the northbound convoy all hands would dive into the canal and have a swim. The temperature was getting real warm; we had been issued with topees and warned if we were caught out on deck without our topee on we would be logged without hesitation. When the northbound convoy approached all hands would reboard and prepare to continue the voyage south. Unfortunately I couldn't swim and the more I shouted for help the more the old man got annoyed. Eventually the penny dropped he realized I couldn't swim. Two sailors were dispatched from the ship to help me sparkle back onboard.

When I arrived onboard I was in front of the captain and called for every low creature under the sun. I was threatened with instant flogging if I hadn't learned to swim by the end of the voyage. When we entered the Red Sea from the Gulf of Suez the weather was just so hot I was sure I would die. When I went to the bridge at night to practise signalling my lips cracked with the heat. I saw a light some distance away, which the third officer ordered me to call. When I did call it's funnel became a blaze of colour. Some large liners did that, they switched on their funnel floodlights, showing off their size really when called by another vessel. The ship I called happened to be the famous French liner "*PASTEUR* "she was bound from Saigon to Marseille with French troops on their way home after fighting in Indo-China. Some nine days after leaving the canal we arrived at Ras Tanura where there is absolutely nothing but desert sand. Stephen and I walked along the shore to watch some Arabs spear fish. A couple of Arabs were playing what we would call drafts they invited us to join them which we did. Early the next morning we completed loading nearly 16,000 tons of crude oil for Rotterdam. The voyage to Rotterdam was just like the outward-bound voyage except tank cleaning was not required or possible as we were full of cargo.

When passing round Ras el Hadd on the Oman coast the captain drew our attention to a wrecked ship on the coast. This was the famous British tramp steamer 'Baron Inverclyde' which ran aground there just after the First World War. When help eventually arrived the crew were all found dead with their throats cut. The cliffs and the hills along the coast looked most foreboding but there was something majestic about the various shades of reds and yellows in the colour of their scenery.

Upon visiting the duty free shops in Rotterdam how we wished we earned a little more money. Next voyage we would endeavour to earn some more money by perhaps making sea bags and canvas covers for the engineer's personal radios or any other equipment, which needed a cover whilst travelling. Rotterdam was just a big industrial seaport with nothing to see but ships and mountains of various colours of iron ore. It was strange to see so many little hamlets scattered among the engineering plants and mountains of raw material. It did not take long to discharge our cargo and for us to get underway again.

This time we were bound for Abadan on the Shatt el Arab river in Iran. Upon arrival after the usual tank cleaning etc we had engine trouble and so were put on a repair berth for about ten days. The time in port was devoted to assisting the third mate overhaul all the life-saving equipment and lifeboats on the ship. Shore leave was permitted which was most enjoyable. Visits to the Gymkhana Club and the use of the pool were allowed under strict instructions. If we tried to chat up any of the girls we would be thrown out of the club in no uncertain manner. We were given to understand that the girls were Armenian and some ex-pats wives. The Armenian girls were really beautiful it was impossible almost to refrain from speaking to them. The club was a beautiful place to go at night for a drink. Provided one was properly dressed one was made very welcome. Although I found the ex-pats to be rather snooty. Here we had the wives of these workers inclined to look upon us with distain. Though the men themselves were keen to entertain us. I suppose someone different to have a yarn with.

There were many rumours going about and talk of much political discord between the Iranians and the British. A local minister called Musaddiq was endeavouring to get the British out the country and nationalize the oil industry. After completion of loading we were delayed. The local labour refused to let our ropes go and the tugs were having difficulty getting to us to assist with the unberthing. With the fast flowing river if we used our crew to let the rope go they would never be able to jump onboard the ship would move off the berth so quickly. The captain ordered that we would cut the ropes for'ard and swing round to the fast flowing ebb on the stern lines and then cut the after moorings. Full ahead on the engines and provided we got the ropes in quickly so as not to foul the propeller we were away. That is exactly what we did. We got away bound for Las Palmas with a full cargo of bunker oil. Each time a ship stops in Las Palmas for bunkers whilst we were discharging cargo we would have to stop working the cargo, which in turn means a longer stay in Las Palmas for us.

I had spent until August trading between the Persian Gulf ports and North West European ports. It was wonderful when we at last arrived in the UK and berthed in Fawley to be told that I was being relieved. Unfortunately when I arrived home on leave I was advised that I should not have been given leave. It was the company rule that a first year cadet must do at least one year of service before being granted leave. I had been given leave through an administration error. However I was given one months leave after which I would join another ship the 'Esso Bristol' on which I would have to serve for at least one year. The other cadet Stephen had had enough of the sea and so resigned.

After a wonderful leave I was ordered to join the "Esso Bristol" in Grangemouth on the 6th. October 1950. Upon completion of discharge we sailed for the Dutch Antilles, Aruba. We had to go to a repair berth on arrival in Aruba to have engine repairs carried out. The trip down to Aruba was beautiful weather wise. The harbour master was a friend of the father of the senior cadet, my new shipmate, Charlie. On arrival at San Nicholas, Aruba we were made most welcome. The harbour masters wife had just given birth to a baby boy. The following night there was a great party in the big Esso club were we all wet the babies head. (Little did I know that in years to come that same baby would serve first as my second officer and later as my chief officer when I was a captain).

Our next port of call was New York or really Perth Amboy. Charlie and I were given shore leave. We were both keen to see New York so we took the shuttle (Local train) into Pen' Street station New York. On the train from Perth Amboy to New York the whole ambiance of the place looked as if nobody had any interest in the place. Town planning seemed to be totally lacking it looked as if a giant had just lifted a handful of houses and thrown them anywhere. Everywhere seemed to be a mess. The British Cadets Club on Seventh Avenue made us most welcome. This is a club, which was opened by two English Ladies during the Second World War for the entertainment of British Cadets. It was well known that cadets were paid very low wages. At the club we were given a large slice of chocolate gateau cake and a tin of coke all much appreciated. Upon leaving the club we endeavoured to find our way via the New York subway to East 47th.Street and the 'Rodesand Bar' to meet some American Naval Cadets from the American Naval Academy at Annapolis. I had met these cadets when last on leave. They were visiting Belfast with the United States Fleet at that time.

We left Perth Amboy for Caripito, in Venezuela. Caripito is far into the jungles of South America. In order to turn in the narrow river San Juan where it is situated it is necessary to ram the bow up onto the river bank and let the fast flowing river turn the ship. In doing so the bow crashes into the trees of the jungle causing all the birds to take to the air making a dreadful racket as they squealed together with all the monkeys. The kaleidoscope of colour of all the birds was really magnificent. After berthing we cadets were taken to a jungle hut of some kind and given a glass of coke and then shown out side to look over a railing to some old logs. On these logs crawled the largest snakes I ever saw. We were told they were anacondas.

The cargo was loaded quickly when we were soon underway again bound for Antwerp, which turned out to be a most interesting city. A bus was laid on to take the crew to town and to collect them at the main railway station to take them back to the ship in the evening. One of the bars we frequented had a dance band, which was operated entirely by robots and was really excellent to dance to. As young cadets do we each obtained a longhaired dictionary and endeavoured to learn the language.

Upon completion of discharge we sailed in ballast for Sidon in the Lebanon to load for New York again. On the passage across the Atlantic we received a dreadful hammering from a storm. It was stormy during the whole passage to New York. The captain hove too for three days. That is he kept the ships head up into the wind and slowed the ship down with just enough power on the engines to maintain steerageway. The storm damage was very extensive. Having lost a lifeboat and the whole of the for'ard flying bridge and part of the cargo manifold. That is were the cargo pipelines are connected to the ship to facilitate discharging and loading the cargo. Upon completion of discharge we gas freed and then moved to a repair berth. Having spent all our subs we had no money whatsoever; nobody liked to lend cadets money. Cadets were known to be poorer than church mice but we did go for walks in the neighbourhood until one of the locals advised it was not the area to be walking about in especially at night. Not the place for two young lads especially strangers on their own.

Eventually we sailed for Punta Cardon, Venezuela to load for Aruba our orders delighted us until we learned that we would load in Punta Cardon and do about twenty trips between Punta Cardon and Aruba. It is only a few hours steaming between the two ports. The chief officer explained that we would have to assist the officers greatly and accept considerable responsibility for the loading and discharging of the cargo. With sea watches and cargo watches if we could keep the pace it would be a real trial of our ability. Shore leave was totally out of the question. We completed so many trips that I lost count but I believe it was almost thirty. Eventually we loaded in Aruba for Hamburg with the promise that we would be given all the time in Hamburg off as a reward for the work we did trading between Aruba and Punta Cardon.

On arrival Hamburg we disappeared of to catch the ferry to Saint Pauli to sample the Repperbahn and see the sights we had heard so much about but didn't really believe existed. We came upon the Winkle Strasse, which was boarded up at the entrance with exception of a small doorway. This area was out of bounds to HM Forces but not to merchant seamen. It should have been out of bounds to humanity and the dogs in the street. On the trip back down the river to our ship I was totally exhausted and fell fast asleep on the little ferry. The next day was a beautiful sunny Sunday afternoon. My shipmate Charlie and I decided to have one last run ashore and so caught the ferry up to town and went for a walk by the lakes in the city centre. The numbers of yachts with beautiful coloured sails and girls dressed in bright colours was a sight to behold. Shore leave ended at 2100 hence it was time to get back to the ship. Our orders were for Texas City to load Aviation Spirit for the American Air Force. We had come under charter to the United States Maritime Commission in other words the American Armed Forces.

The captain sent for me

"I have the results of The Merchant Navy Training Boards First Year Examination Papers". You will have to work harder. I notice you are not as quick as you might be in your basic mathematics. I will give you some advice young man. Enrol with the Seafarers Education Service known as the 'College of the Sea'. Ask for their special course in mathematics. "You are going to have to become more advanced in your mathematics and your navigation. Spherical trigonometry and stereographic projections will require much effort on your part. However, you'll get their son, you're a good worker".

We loaded in Texas City and had a great time ashore with the local High School girls. I had never seen a High School band before. I think the boys I was with were mesmerised with the cheer girls leading the band. There seemed to be a big school practise event-taking place. Everyone in town was keen to know what part of the world we were from. I really think some folk thought we were from outer space.

I completed more than a year on the 'Esso Bristol', which I found very difficult but even to this day the thoughts of that year, bring back many good memories. The fact that we had to do so much longer than the other crewmembers before being granted leave I think perhaps was why most officers were rather kind to us. Maybe that was the reason I was allowed to keep my monkey, wee Joey, as a pet. One problem I did experience when arriving home on leave was that ones friends at home made their own lives and their own new friends. It was difficult to make a new circle of friends. Ones friends knew that as soon as your month's leave was up you would be away and forget about them. Murphy's law always worked that you would meet a nice girl the last week of your leave that would have forgotten about you by the first week of your voyage.

Once another cadet, a friend of mine home on leave and I went to a dance were we met two girls. Needless to say we asked if we could leave them home. I wasn't happy at all when I heard where my friend was going to leave his girl. I told him he was mad Belfast being what it was at that period. We were both in uniform, which wasn't a very clever thing to be wearing in the area my friend was taking his girl to. He told me in no uncertain terms that I was bigoted and ignorant, so I left him to it. Next day when

I called at his house his mother demanded to know what we had been doing the previous night. Whilst my friend had been up an alleyway a bomb went off round the corner from were he was endeavouring to make love. He left the wee girl and run like hell half way across Belfast to get home. What had really happened was the IRA had thrown a bomb at the local Police Station, where he had been round the corner courting. After what I had been saying to him. He thought they had thrown the bomb at him.

I joined my next ship the "Esso Bedford" which was an old ship with which there seemed to be much trouble especially engine trouble. I joined her at Fawley after an exhausting journey from Belfast by ferry and then train from Liverpool via London. On completion of discharge we proceeded to Banias in Syria to load back to Fawley thence to Mena-El-Ahmedi for L.E.F.O. meaning 'Lands. End. For. Orders'. My period of working with the crew on deck was finished I now commenced watch keeping with the chief officer keeping proper watches on the bridge and learning so much. The first time he allowed me to take an azimuth that is get a bearing of a star and then calculate the bearing mathematically and compare the two bearings to find the error on the compass. When the chief officer told me to log it in the compass observation book I thought I had really made it. My navigation was being trusted which meant real progress was being made. I completed many voyages to the Persian Gulf and various ports in the Mediterranean and Western Europe.

On passage through the Red Sea the ships two main engines stopped and couldn't be started again. The engineers were working on the main engine inside the crankcase. The electrician who was rigging lights in the crankcase fell into the crankcase tearing the much of his throat out. He was carried along to the ships hospital and medical locker. The captain was called who together with the chief steward and the chief officer worked on the electrician's throat. I ran messages back and forward to the bridge and radio-room The captain had ordered a Pan Pan Pan message to be sent to all ships. That is a call for help to all ships. The troopship 'Empire Orwell' who was homeward bound from Korea with commandos answered our call. A rendezvous was made with the 'Empire Orwell' who offered to put her doctor onboard. That was a relief to all hands we were now going to get professional help for our electrician.

We were coming into that time of the year when the SW Monsoons are sometimes felt in the Red Sea. The wind was strong and the sea quite rough. The engineers had managed to get one engine working. Just at that time the 'Empire Orwell' suggested that we use our lifeboat to transfer the patient to them as their doctor may wish to keep the patient onboard. We anticipated rendezvousing in about thirty hours if we can't get the other engine going. This was all agreed between the two ships. Instead of putting the patient in the ships hospital it was decided to put him in the Chief Stewards cabin where the steward could keep a good watch over him in case he died during the night. The Chief Steward could sleep on the settee in his cabin and the electrician on the bunk. Whilst on watch I was sent every half hour to check that the electrician was still in this world and report back to the bridge. In the darkness of the cabin I felt the pulse of the wee man on the bunk. As daylight broke I soon discovered that I had been testing the pulse of the steward not the electrician. The steward had decided to take the bunk and put lecky on the settee.

When the captain and the chief officer were planning the transfer I overheard the captain tell the chief officer to take the cadet with him. I could look after the patient in the lifeboat and keep him comfortable furthermore it would be good experience for me. Every time I looked out at the sea running and listened to the noise of the wind and rain I thought it was really an experience I could do without. We spotted the "Empire Orwell" through the rain. She signalled to us "*Suggest you proceed on passage to Port Sudan to repatriate your patient to the UK. Weather too bad for transfer*". The engineers were soon able to get the other engine going, it wasn't long until we were proceeding at full speed a good ten knots bound for Port Sudan to land our injured electrician.

At the anchorage of Port Sudan whilst the injured electrician was being taken ashore to hospital

I was looking down into the sea. The biggest fish I ever saw just broke the surface with it's back. It was a tiger shark a real monster rather frightening to be so close to. Once again we were underway making our way down the Red Sea. When passing Aden the captain received a signal from the doctor at the hospital in Port Sudan congratulating him on the professional manner in which he packed the electricians throat he had saved his life. About two months later when homeward bound we called at Port Sudan and picked up our electrician and took him home to the UK. He looked as though he was suffering from gout. His throat looked swollen somewhat and his voice very weak but other than that he was ok.

I completed many more voyages on Esso tankers. It was now early 1954 and time for me to come ashore to sit for my second officers examination success in which would entitle me to sail as a third officer. It was the practise in those days to hold a qualification of the rank above the rank in which one was engaged. One was entitled to two months study leave to prepare for the examinations. In the event of failure one more month was allowed for a second attempt. Needless to say nearly everyone failed their signals examination to get another months study leave. After one months voyage leave and three months study leave it was rather hard to return to sea. Nearly all my friends were serving in cargo ships or liners. Their stories of good spells in port and decent trade routes made me feel that it was time also

I had a change of ship type.

On completion of my examination I was promoted to the dizzy heights of third officer and ordered to join the "Esso Glasgow" at Southampton. We sailed in ballast for Sidon in the Lebanon to load for New York. The trip to New York was one, which I shall never forget. The cargo pipes were torn from the deck, as was the fo'ard flying bridge during a terrible storm. Having experienced this before I knew we would spend some time in New York having repairs carried out. This meant a few days respite and more shore leave. After the repairs were completed we sailed for Caripito to load again for Fawley. On arrival at Fawley I left "Esso Tankers" and joined the Royal Mail Line.

CHAPTER FIVE

During my last year as a cadet in Esso I kept a bridge watch on my own which was a lot of responsibility it also effectively meant that the ship had four watch-keeping officers. I also felt very good at such trust being placed in me. The Royal Mail line had a rule whereby all officers had to start at the very bottom for me that was fourth officer. A fourth officer was treated as no more than a senior cadet. I found that very hard to accept. Upon joining the "Highland Monarch" as a relieving fourth officer I found my responsibilities to be almost nil.

The public rooms in the old ship were really beautiful. I think the décor was supposed to represent an old Scottish Castle inside though my cabin was supposed to represent a broom cupboard. For a writing desk I had a piece of board to lower over my washbasin and that was the writing desk. I could sit on a little settee and put my feet on the bunk at the other side of the cabin. She loaded in London a general cargo for Rio de Janeiro, Santos, Montevideo and Buenos Aires. Outward bound she took onboard 120 First Class passengers at Tilbury and 500 immigrants at Vigo and Lisbon for various South American ports.

Homeward bound she loaded at the above ports thousands of tons of chilled beef and chilled lamb. Actually she had over half a million cubic feet of refrigerated space and could carry 150,000 carcasses of beef and lamb. The sea passage was about twenty days which was one of the reasons these ships carried so much chilled meat rather than frozen. It was all so different from life on a tanker. The social life onboard was full of rules and regulations, which I found difficult to comprehend, but it had its compensations. Though I did come to grips quite well with always being properly dressed in uniform especially after 1800 in the evening.

I had rather strange hours to keep. In the morning I kept the 4 to 8 watch in the morning I kept a watch from 1300 until 1400 and in the evening the 1700 until 1900. All this watch keeping was as a junior with another senior officer. I had nearly three years watch keeping experience by myself onboard a big tanker. Because I kept odd watch times my times in the dinning saloon were also rather odd. I dinned in the evening in the First Class saloon on my own at a table in the corner like a bad boy at 1900 because I had just come off watch. All the other officers having finished tea by that time, 1900. The passengers and senior officers dinned together at 1900 together at various large tables. They had what appeared to me to be very large decorative menu cards. I had just a little plain menu card as you might have on an ordinary cargo boat.

A beautiful big sweeping staircase was the means of entrance into the saloon. At the bottom of which was usually a long table with various cold meats, salads and glazed poultry and fish. Always in the middle of this lot was a little roast piglet with a lemon in its mouth. One evening it had an orange in its mouth. I swiped the orange out of the pig's mouth and put it in my pocket. All hell was to play, over an orange being pinched from the pig's mouth by an officer. The food left much to be desired in those ships. I thought the time was long gone when passengers in the same saloon as officers would have a different menu to the officers and I do not mean by size but by content that was not to be. After I had been in front of the captain for my little misdemeanour. As I obviously wasn't fitting in to life on a passenger ship he, the captain, suggested that I should try one of the company's cargo liners, which carried just twelve passengers. He offered to have me transferred to one if I so wished upon our return to the UK. I agreed to do just that and joined the 'Loch Gown' for my next voyage she had only made one voyage from new. She was a beautiful ship; because of the London dock strike we loaded in Newport, Wales. All our cargo was sent down to Newport by lorry. Lorries were queued through the town right out into the country. It seemed to take weeks to get the cargo loaded but we enjoyed the spell in Newport. The weather was wonderful and we gave a party for the nurses from the local hospital so everyone got 'boxed of'. The third officer did a deal with an insurance broker. He agreed to take out a Life Insurance Policy if the broker would hire his wee car to us in the evenings, which he agreed to, the car was a little Morris 8. The third officer and I together with our nurses toured the countryside. We had a great night drinking with some RAF officers and their girl friends in a pub in the Wye valley. I thumped the piano sufficiently to let us think we were having a singsong accompanied by a pianist. There was a beautiful old abbey nearby which gave the whole valley a classical air about the place.

Our cargo was for the West Coast of America and Canada. First port of call was Bermuda, which was so expensive we could just about afford a glass of water, next port Kingston, Jamaica. We enjoyed our afternoons by the pool in the Myrtlebank Hotel and the evenings in the 'Glass Slipper Club.' I wasn't considered experienced enough in cargo ships to be allowed to keep a deck watch without a more senior officer on deck, which meant I had a lot of time off in port. I couldn't really complain about that. We passed through the Panama Canal and then up to Los Angelus were I was able to meet a very dear friend from home. She was very kind, making sure that I enjoyed my stay In Los Angelus to the full. When she left the ship and was disembarking she wore the tightest pants ever seen on a young women. The Dockers actually stopped work and came up out of the hatch to watch her go ashore down the gangway; she loved every second of the attention.

In San Francisco Bay we discharged at various berths around the bay, not least of which was the city of Oakland. We then went up the coast to Portland then into Puget Sound to Seattle and Tacoma. Eventually we called at Victoria were we were quite sure they rolled the sidewalks up at night, the place seemed so quiet. A few of us went ashore together, actually walked out into the countryside at night and found what we thought was a church hall from which the music emanating sounded good. In we went and when the girls discovered we were sailors they went over backwards to give us a good time. Actually we had discovered a ceilidh dance. A really a wonderful night was had by all. Our last port was Vancouver were, upon completion of discharge we commenced loading for home Europe, Rotterdam, Antwerp and Hamburg.

At Vancouver I received a letter from my sister telling me she had made arrangements for me, when I would come home on leave next time, to meet a lovely wee girl who had just started work with her. That night some of us went to the British Officers Club, which was in the same building as the YWCA so, one couldn't help not meeting a female. I met a young French Canadian Girl who invited me home to dinner, which was all very nice. Except, her father never spoke to me all night but kept staring at me, it was most un-nerving if not down right uncomfortable. The bugger suddenly barked at me in a rather gruttle voice. Are you a protestant? I barked at him

No! A Bush Baptist. Her sister lent me her car to go for a run up to Queen Elizabeth Park to enjoy the view of the city lights of Vancouver. The view was just magnificent the following night we went to see the show "Annie Get Your Gun" in the open Air Theatre in Stanley Park which has a most beautiful coloured fountain the like of which I had never seen before.

At Vancouver we loaded timber and grain then moved to New Westminster to load cases of tinned salmon. The other ports at which we had discharged we loaded cases of tinned fruit. In the refrigerated holds fresh citrus fruit was stowed. Royal Mail was very keen to show off their relatively new ship. This entailed numerous cocktail parties for shippers and in large ports when social dignitaries were invited the ship would be dressed over all. Everyone was expected to be on their very best behaviour no real drinking encase we might resort to Nautical Gaelic, after 1800 order of the day was number 10's

What a difference from oil tankers it all took considerable getting used to but I still felt like a senior cadet as though I had made little progress career wise and that was not really for me. If I wasn't to get a berth as a third officer I was going to get it elsewhere. The weather compensated somewhat for my moans it was beautiful as we passed down the Californian Coast. The passengers sunbathing by the ships swimming pool. I acting the smart guy and trying to swim dived into the pool and immediately got into difficulties. The slight roll of the ship made the waves in the pool bigger than usual, which added to my difficulties. Luckily the passengers realized my problems were for real and rescued me from the pool. Never did I feel so humiliated in all my life. The look on the other officers faces every time I went near them said enough. I never got over the humiliation nor did I ever learn to swim. Believe me it wasn't for the want of trying.

After bunkering at Curacao we shaped a course for home when I told the captain that I wished to look for a different company after I had had my leave. I found Royal Mail rather stuffy I had no wish to sail as a fourth officer having qualified to sail as a second officer. Soon I would be home when I would have to think just what I was going to do about getting promotion. In the meantime I had more important matters to attend too. On a miserable wet night in Belfast I was wondering what to do with myself when my sister suggested that I get myself up to the home of the young girl she wrote to me about. I thought to myself yes why not.

"Ok" said I. "Give me her address, what did you say her name was Sheelagh what? If this is some joke it will back fire on you and I will make sure it does."

"If you take yourself up there remember she is a friend of mine so behave yourself." "Aye ok, I'm away."

As I sat on the bus I thought I must have been losing my senses making a cold call on a wee girls door like this. Anyway lets see what she is like. I arrived at her door, gave it a rather gentle knock and a rather attractive young lady opened the door wearing awful looking slippers with a tweed skirt and a yellow blouse, I said.

"Hello Sheelagh I'm Ralph" she said.

"Yes I know, won't you come in" she replied.

I just thanked her and walked into her home. Surprise, surprise sitting there was another young lady I knew. As one would know Northern Ireland isn't the size of a decent farm in some countries. Anyway we had a great evening yarning. I invited Sheelagh out in my best western ocean accent a fact I have never, in half a centaury, been allowed to forget, because actually I married her.

I thought it might be a good Idea to join a ship trading into Belfast on a regular basis because I wanted to get to know Sheelagh better. If I returned immediately to the Foreign Going trade she might meet someone else whilst I was on a longer voyage. I decided to stay on the coast for a little while and get to know her properly.

I joined this little ship in Liverpool, which was loading for Belfast I thought it was my lucky day straight home again. She was lying alongside another ship, which I had to cross over to get to my little coaster. I looked over the side of this Shaw Saville Liner at my wee coaster and thought. "God this woman had better be worth this." I threw my gear onboard, my sea bag landed on the deck with a thump. From such a height my bag sounded like the 'A bomb' the deck it landed on was the deck head of the captains cabin. That was me in his bad books before I even got onboard. He came out of his cabin like something demented looking for the culprit. I received a polite grunt when I introduced myself to him. At lunch the cook gave me a bowl of soup with a slice of bread what looked like a bread cart. I hope you like soup there is not much else. Said the cook "Watch that table cloth second mate, the old man hasn't read it yet." I thought this would take a bit of getting used to. Anyway if I couldn't take a joke I suppose I shouldn't have signed on.

Looking at the cargo I thought we are not going to be very long in Belfast. Just a couple tractors to be discharged from the deck and then across to Glasgow. We arrived in Belfast at 0900 on Wednesday morning and sailed again at noon for Glasgow arriving at 0100 next morning. I didn't see Sheelagh at all. Whilst steaming down the Clyde bound for Liverpool there was an old sailor man at the wheel on my watch. He kept looking at me and I knew he wanted to tell me something. Eventually he said, "Second mate you know on the coast we keep the wheelhouse doors closed, not like foreign going where they keep the doors open. On that little ship it was the practice to send the helmsman below to put a few shovels of coal on the boggey to keep the heat up in the accommodation when at sea. Thinking I would do well in the coastal trade if I tried I sent the helmsman below to stoke the boggey up and closed the wheelhouse doors. It wasn't long until I thought we had run into fog. In the darkness of the night visibility seemed very low, I couldn't see out of the wheelhouse windows and was just about to start the whistle blowing when a big tanker blew her whistle. I opened the wheelhouse door; run onto the bridge and soon discovered the ruddy wheelhouse windows were all steamed up. The stars looked beautiful with a big moon beginning to shine between the hilltops of the Clyde. I was really glad I hadn't called the old man, which were standing orders in any ship approaching fog. On reflection I thought better to do a decent voyage and have a longer leave and get better paid. In fact better to sail in the ships you felt more at home in. This wee ship is fine if you live in Liverpool but a dead loss if you live in Ireland. Sometimes she would get four hours in Belfast. I stayed in the ship about four weeks. At the end of the month I decided as soon as we berth in Liverpool I will look for a decent ship.

On arrival Liverpool I went up to the offices of the Harrison Line and obtained a berth as third officer. They seemed pleased to see me. Yes, join the "Adviser" in London next week was my orders; she will be bound in ballast for Manati, Cuba to load a full cargo of sugar for Liverpool. It was important to get down there quickly and get loaded because Cuba was in political turmoil. The country was experiencing a guerrilla war and Fidel Castro who was fighting just to the east of Manati trying to take over the country. He was expected to take Manati soon. Although we were an old ship we could make thirteen knots maybe a little more at a push with our Bauer-Wack turbine.

We made a good passage down to Cuba. The stevedores only worked in the morning finishing about noon. Loading was carried out by cutting open the bags of sugar and pouring the sugar down into the holds. Bleeding the bags was what this method of loading was known as. This slow antiquated operation took us nearly three weeks to load. It didn't really worry us we were all enjoying ourselves on the beautiful beaches in the sun. Sunday there was no cargo working so we decided to go picnicking with a few cases of beer and a few roast chickens. Before entering the sea, which was by a lovely bay one of the engineers enquired of the locals if it was safe to swim in the local water. They assured us, very safe no problems. When we had returned to the ship after a great day ashore and in the middle of having our tea there was terrible commotion on the quayside. Our West Indian crew had just caught a very large hammerhead shark. This monster put paid to any further ideas of swimming in the sea. One rather quaint ritual the local girls all had was to bring their fathers or husbands or who ever their breakfast on the ship. This operation was carried out every morning about nine o'clock when all hands could each find an excuse to be in the area of the gangway about that time. Watching the girls deliver a carafe of wine and what appeared to be a loaf of bread to their men folk was a most interesting past time. Compensating a little for our lack of swimming.

I was going home to be married. On the passage home we ran into a real storm South West of the Azores causing us to lie hove too until the weather improved. No way was I going to make my wedding so I sent a wireless message to change the date for the wedding. Unfortunately the "Adviser" was an old ship and was only fitted with an MF radio hence messages had to be relayed via another ship if we were not close to a commonwealth coast station. Needless to say a cockup over the dates was made in the relaying of the message. I did eventually get home with a day to spare to get married. The wedding took place in time to let us go on honeymoon for a week. On arrival home from our honeymoon I was immediately transferred to the "Selector" sailing from London to the West Indies calling at every island in the West Indies except the French Islands. Discharging was carried out southbound through the islands and northbound loading for home was completed in Barbados for London. I was going home to college to sit my Chief Officers examinations and enjoy three months study leave.

On the success of my examinations I was promoted to second officer and joined the "Astronomer" in London bound for the West Indies and the Spanish Main. At La Guaira, Venezuela I had an accident injuring my back and ending up in hospital. A revolution broke out whilst hospitalised in La Guaira, which included severe rioting. The captain was most reluctant to leave me in the hospital; the agent also suggested that if he could he should take me out of the country. The captain thank God, sent the chief officer to get me out of the hospital as soon as he did so and got me onboard we sailed. I was very lucky to be serving a kind and thoughtful captain. He put into Aruba at Oranjestad and had me taken to hospital again. When completing the paper work for admittance to the hospital I was asked my religion. I answered the nun "Church of Ireland" which was the truth. She wouldn't have that and insisted in writing on the forms "Roman Catholic" of course I was having none of that. The hospital had first, second and third class wards, I was lucky I was in the first class. The morning after my admittance a priest arrived at my bedside to advise me that I was a Roman Catholic and that I would be expected to be at mass on Christmas night. He and I had very strong words on the subject. Notwithstanding the fact that I was not to move, ordered by the doctors to lie flat at all times. Two nuns arrived just before midnight at my bedside with my clothes ordering me to get dressed, we were going to mass. "Like hell we are," said I. needless to say we didn't. The next day the priest again arrived at my bed and enquired about my family, how many children I had. At that time I had one boy where upon my spiritual mentor proceeded to give me a lecturer on having more children. By this time I had enough of this gentleman, but the nuns never gave up suggesting

I was maybe a lost Catholic. I just could not explain to them that not everyone in Ireland was Catholic.

During the night another patient arrived to share the room with me who was a chief officer from a Norwegian tanker. I was given to understand that he had a mental breakdown of some sort. I felt that the nuns were giving him a rough time in as much as they always seem to be shouting at him. When the Norwegian consul called to see him I reported to him that I felt the nuns were rather rough with him. A couple of doctors and what I assumed to be senior nuns had a sort of case conference by his bedside. When their voices became raised I intervened and was told to mind my own business or I too would be removed from the hospital. They arrived back during the early hours of the morning, gave him an injection and immediately removed him. I asked what was going on and was told to shut up and go asleep. There were a couple of Norwegian ratings in the second-class wards to whom I reported what had happened. Soon the Norwegian consul came to see me asking if I would make a statement about the incident. "Yes sure I will" if you get the British consul to call with me, which he did. The ships agent also called and between them I was sent home. Eventually the only seamen left in the hospital were a few from the Indian sub-continent who seemed to be totally mystified by all the upheaval in the hospital.

I was flown to Maracabo were I again visited a

hospital my back being very painful after the bumpy flight from Aruba. It was decided to get me home by sea for whatever reason I do not know. One of our ships was in La Salinas, which I was put onboard, bound for Liverpool. After a rather most uncomfortable trip I eventually arrived in Belfast. There was nothing the hospital could do for me but have me rest. To expedite my physiotherapy an ambulance called at my home at regular intervals to take me to and from hospital for treatment. Whilst lying at home I developed severe ulcers in my mouth preventing me eating solids. I could only take liquids. My diet consisted of Guinness and raw eggs mixed together in a bowl, a lovely remedy, strongly recommended. After a couple of months lying on my back I was fit again and reported for sea service. I never thought I would be so glad to get back to sea again after my experiences.

CHAPTER SIX

My ship the "Astronomer" had been transferred to the East African run when we loaded in Glasgow and Birkenhead for Port Said, Port Sudan, and Aden. In the lower holds we had hundreds of tons of military equipment for the army fighting the Mau in Kenya. Fighting had broken out in the Radian Mountains in the Yemen to which many of the military units fighting in Kenya were transferred. Having much of their equipment in our lower holds for discharge at Mombassa and was now required in Aden we had to discharge the t'ween decks to get their armoured cars, scout cars and water bowers out from the ships holds at Aden. The extra work necessitated a longer stay in Aden of all places. The military advised us to guard the ship and trust no one as they expected an uprising. Good for the British Army they had the means to guard themselves and the men to do it. We had a few sailors with a piece of stick who were quick with their fists and more likely to start a war. When we left Aden to continue our voyage to Mogadicio, Mombassa, Tanga, Zanzibar, Pemba and Dar-es- Salaam we were a very happy crew even though we had severe out breaks of illness from time to time among the whole ships company. This we believed to be due to something the boys had picked up in the swimming pool ashore in Port Sudan. All hands were put on light diets and a good dose of stomach powder every four hours. The severe ones a couple of anti-allergy tablets twice a day. They all lived for another day, the chief officer was hospitalised in Mombassa to have Kidney stones removed which was an excuse for the other officers to visit the hospital and get to know different people. We were made most welcome at the gymkhana club in Dar-es-Salaam. They had an extensive program of social events to which we were always invited including trips to various places. Unfortunately I always seemed to be engaged in some duty or other. Though looking at the state some of the boys were in when they returned to the ship I was usually most pleased to have missed the particular outing. They always had very large bites all over their bodies including their eyelids causing the most severe pain. Those who didn't go on the trips were convinced the lads were only suffering from local love bites.

At long last we headed up the East African Coast homeward bound. Loading commenced in the same ports we had discharged at as we came south. The bulk of the cargo comprised of tobacco, sisal, all manner of spices, cattle cake, and hides, ground nuts and copper ingots for Avonmouth, Belfast and Liverpool. We had been away four months, I must say a most interesting four months As we pulled alongside the berth in Belfast my wife and little boy came forward to give me a big hug. I was so proud of little David he was just coming to grips with walking. His afternoon onboard was spent crawling up and down the ships alleyways. The customs charged 75p duty on the little performing toy I had for the child and the little music box I had for my wife. I thought how mean can these people become. Especially the manner in which they enjoy their free tots.

After my leave I joined the "ss Prospector" bound for Barbados just before sailing from Barbados I took unwell. I was taken to a doctor who suggested I saw another doctor. The elderly doctor then suggested that I come down to his garden shed or as he called it his examination room. The shed had to be seen to be believed. The old boy rolled out a mattress, which was all stained and suggested I lie on it whilst he examined me. He touched my stomach, scratched his chin, chased some chickens of a shelf above my head, looked at me and then made a gargantuan decision. "Young man" said he "I think we'll have you admitted you to hospital where they know more about these things than I do" I was off to hospital, next a little West Indian nurse commenced to shave my pubic hair in preparation for the knife. This gave her tremendous fun so much so that she called her many friends to see a white mans pubic hair being shaved. It is not the black tight little curls like that of a Blackman but soft.

When I came out of the anaesthetic I told the

nurse I had had a dream that my mother had died. In my dream a man told me. She said, "Your mama is dead Mr Potts she is. The agent called with a radio message from your brother to say your mama is dead." I was still feeling very drowsy and couldn't quite take it in that she was dead after all the years of illness. None of the company's ships calling at Barbados had spare accommodation onboard to facilitate a passage home for me. When I was discharged from hospital I was accommodated at the Aquatic Club until such times as a suitable ship called at Bridgetown and gave me a passage home.

Life at the Aquatic Club was most idyllic. Someone had put a notice in the local paper to the effect that an Irish second officer had been hospitalised from the Harrison Liner "Prospector."

After that notice appeared in the paper I had numerous visitors to my bedside. Including those who prayed so hard for me and called on the Lord to visit me that they scared the living daylights out of me, I actually got under the bedclothes. I don't know what they may have done to the good Lord had he come to see me. I was surprised how many Irish people came to visit me. One gentleman who owned a garage lent me a car for the period I was on the island. I had endless invitations to dinner and outings to shoot water crabs. I really did wish I could swim, many people offered to teach me which I accepted but alas, a total waste of time. Eventually I got a passage home had some leave and joined my next ship. An old liberty ship the "Statesman" bound for South Africa and Mozambique. Quite sometime was spent in the South African ports during which time the South African Apartheid Police harassed us very often. They would come onboard at night demanding to search the ship looking for Cape Coloured Girls, many of whom were beautiful, checking to see if they were with white ships officers. Our crew were black West Indians to whom they didn't object being with the local girls. I made many trips on the "Statesman" to South Africa, The Spanish Main and Central America including Mexico and the American Gulf Ports. Having completed two years actual seatime since sitting my Chief Officers examinations, which was the qualifying time necessary to sit for a Master's Certificate I applied to go on study leave again.

It was my intention to become one of the highest qualified seamen in the Merchant Navy but this would be very costly. It required two years ashore in College without pay, studying for the examinations for an Extra Masters Certificate. As I had by this time two young children I began to think that perhaps I just could not afford to put myself through college. Qualifying meant the possibility of a good shore job and I did want more time with the family. I did obtained my Masters Certificate and was awarded The Mature State Scholarship to help me do Part 'A' and the Orals of the Extra Masters Certificate. At the end of it all I was stoney broke and had to return to sea in order to earn more money to carry on studying at college.

The chief marine superintendent, when I applied to join a ship congratulated me on my examination successes and enquired, "Do you intend to carry on and sit for part 'B' of your Extras"

I replied, "Yes of course".

"Well" said he "What we really want in our ships, are good experienced and knowledgeable young officers of which you are one? We do not want Oxford Dons, Give up all this studying and return to you ship. You have a great career ahead of you in this company (they no longer exist to-day) if you just give up all this bookwork. I have an Extra Masters Certificate, which I obtained in a German Prison of War Camp but it hasn't opened, up the world for me. Go away and think all about it and let me know what you want to do. That is exactly what I did. A couple of the younger superintendents advised me strongly to keep at it. I had come too far and worked too hard to give it all up at this stage. This I did, I received a very nice letter by return of post advising me they did not have a berth for me. "Sorry Ralph".

Luckily I only had to make a phone call and I had a berth as Chief Officer in a bulk carrier the "Clarkeden" which I joined at Workington bound for Narvik. The trip to the artic was rough and very cold. Navigating the fiords in heavy snowstorms was difficult. There was quite a queue of ships waiting to load, which meant anchoring to wait our turn to load. It was quite a place and worth a run ashore. A few of us went ashore up to the restaurant at the top of the chair lift. The view was spectacular the way people were staring at us, I think we were spectacular. We really did look stupid up a snow lift in what was really our Sunday best. Our captain was a tight fisted bugger. He would only allow each man to have a five-pound sub whoever they were which caused quite some friction between he and I. Under no circumstances would he allow anyone to have more. It cost £1 to go ashore in the launch and £1 return leaving £3 to spend. My £3 was spent on a pair of sealskin slippers for my wife and that was that. I suppose the old man was wise really. Everything is exorbitantly expensive and not really worth buying. They say the captain is next to God maybe he thought he was God and was protecting us from our stupid ways. We were soon alongside and loaded for Port Talbot. The passage home was wild with the decks constantly awash and the remainder of the ship covered in ice.

Just north of the Shetlands during the morning watch. I observed a ship with all her lights on derricks rigged and working over the side. I felt very strongly that we should report what this ship was about. She was definitely Russian but our captain was not in the least bit interested. After discharge we had orders for Kirkness, which is up at the Russian border between Norway and Russian. During the next eight months we made many trips to the Northern Artic Ports. The

Russians treated us as though we came from Mars. Under no circumstances were we to allow the guards on the gangway to have any chocolate or coca-cola and definitely no cigarettes. A very bossy female agent gave these instructions during the ships clearance. Our chief steward asked of the agent. "Was this the country of equals"?

"Of course it is" she replied.

"Then why are the guards on the gangway not permitted to receive anything from the ship at all, yet you are helping yourself to all of our whiskey and more if you can get it."

"Ah Mr steward we have our rules, you have yours, let us respect each others rules."

I was pleased to get away from Russia much as I find Russia an intriguing country. It is a cold barren god forgiven place in which even the people appear miserable and dowdy. The whole populace looks totally forlorn among their endless blocks of grey miserable flats. After a run ashore in the place one usually comes back onboard feeling depressed. There are some beautiful buildings I suppose, but the endless dilapidated buildings in their vicinity swamp them. Perhaps there are some beautiful buildings in the more historical cities but miles upon miles of dilapidated flats swamp their beauty.

Our orders were to discharge at Irlm on the Manchester ship canal. Upon completion of discharge at Irlm we proceeded down the Manchester Ship Canal bound for Pepal in Sierra Leone to load Iron Ore for Rotterdam. I spent some seven months trading between the world's ore mines and the steel producing ports of Europe. Sagunta in Spain was most pleasant as we always had about ten days loading. The stevedores only worked a quota which they usually finished by noon. The rest of the day could be spent on the beach or just exploring the local town. At the weekend one could take the bus to Valencia a thirty-minute ride away.

After my leave I joined the "Clarkeforth" as chief officer. She was a beautiful ship no cost was spared in fitting out the accommodation. The furnishings and décor in the officers smoke room made it appear and feel like an expensive city club. When I joined her she had just arrived from Australia with grain. We sailed form London to load phosphates in Tampa, Florida for Niigata, Sagata, Kushiro and Hachinohe in Japan. On completion of discharge we sailed for Portland, Oregon to load a full cargo of grain for Mokpo and Masan in Korea. Just before arrival in Korea we had orders from the charters who in fact were the United States government not to deliver the cargo it hadn't been paid for. The charters did not have in their possession a Bill of Lading hence had no means of claiming the cargo. All hell broke loose onboard. The customs came onboard together with the police and various officials demanding their cargo. Still we refused to let them have the cargo without a bill of lading.

That evening four government officials came onboard and invited the captain and myself out for the evening to a geisha house. What a boring night, we sat on our hunkers as wee geisha girls made figures for us out of silver paper, and then they performed dances to music that would make you scream. Next they gave us money to play cards with. I think the message was getting through to them that we were not becoming soft in anyway. The Koreans stood up and indicated that we should follow them. We all ended up in a brothel. Wee girls, in fact children were presented to us at this point our captain went berserk, demanding that we be taken back to our ship. The officials were so sorry and embarrassed, grovelling to us that the whole episode became most annoying and disturbing. Next morning we still refused to let them have their grain. That afternoon a couple of very important gentlemen came onboard with the bill of lading. Power was put on the deck, hatches opened and the stevedores were invited to take their grain. Then commenced the demand for free cigarettes from us at every minute of the day. On one occasion just before breakfast the bos'un called me imploring me to come and see the goings on of the stevedores on the poop deck. (The poop deck is were we kept the forty-gallon drums of swill from the galley, which was emptied when we got to sea). The stevedores were fighting among themselves to get at the swill to eat it. I felt quite sick at the sight of these men and women behaving like animals. I really felt so sorry for them. When they commenced to litterly steal the cargo by tying the bottom of their trousers and the cuffs of their coats. This action made their apparel into bags. They then began filling their trousers and jackets with the grain from the cargo. One felt like helping them. In those days Korea was not the country it is today.

After Korea we came on charter to the Japanese Liner Company NYK and spent the remainder of our time in the Pacific trading from the western seaboard to the eastern seaboard of the Pacific. It seemed as though we had called in every port and island in the Pacific many of which I cannot remember their names. At the end of the charter I was asked would I like a present of silk for my wife. "Of course that would be most appreciated" I replied. As we were moored to buoys in Yokohama harbour a launch was necessary to get ashore. Next morning I was taken ashore to be met by a young Japanese girl on the quayside who took me to a silk warehouse. As we walked around the warehouse she suggested that I would also need a lining of silk for a dress or suit, I told her I would be guided by her. Even I could see the material was just beautiful as it was being beautifully parcelled. I was so pleased with it I couldn't wait to get home to show it to Sheelagh my wife.

We left Yokohama bound for Los Angeles where we were to pay off and travel home via New York. I had all the tickets for the ships crew travelling home via TWA to New York and KLM to Prestwick. I found a barbers shop in Prestwick, when I climbed into the barbers chair I fell fast asleep. I was away nearly a year Heather my daughter was born just before I sailed from London and now she was walking, I couldn't wait to see her. My bags were full of presents, as I had sent my gear home by sea including a Nagoya dinner service, which arrived home exactly in many pieces one year later. A dressmaker one of Belfast's greatest was recommended to make the dress for Sheelagh the silk for which was so tenderly obtained and transported home. Needless to say Murphy's Law prevailed a total and complete mess was made of the dress to such an extent that it has never been worn.

CHAPTER SEVEN

My ship was sold whilst I was on leave as was her sister ship. The company, which operated her, was only a management company and unfortunately lost the management of a number of other ships. I could see the writing on the wall with management shipping companies so I didn't really wish to continue in their employment. Until I found something more suitable I took a job in a little coaster trading from Newry to Liverpool. Whilst in Liverpool I paid a visit to Canadian Pacific Steamships and was immediately offered a berth as third officer provided I did at least one voyage in the junior rank of third officer before promotion to the more senior ranks. After obtaining a berth as third officer I was immediately promoted to second officer and very soon to relieving first officer. That was very fast promotion for a passenger ship in those days.

Although Canadian Pacific was like Royal Mail a passenger ship company what "bull" there was seemed sensible and acceptable. Or perhaps I was more mature and experienced than my days with the Royal Mail. Were "bull" seemed all part of an act at times and rather stupid. For example on Sunday morning an entry was put in the logbook "Magazines inspected and arms found correct" or words to that effect. What arms? When entering ports another entry was "Chained manned." Who manned what chains? Anyway whatever the reason I settled in very well with Canadian Pacific unlike when I joined the Royal Mail Line. On day of arrival and day of sailing also on a Sunday, an officer was not expected to dress for dinner in full mess kit. Also after 1800 in the evening mess kit was not required if watch keeping. Second officers and equivalent rank were expected to have two dinners outward and two dinners homeward likewise two luncheons with the tourist class passengers. The routine for this required a purserette or other female officer and an officer; both in dress uniform to create an entrance. They met at the top of the sweeping staircase, which led into the dinning saloon. The officer would then lead the female officer on his arm into dinner. The passengers appreciated this little show as a little touch of finesse. (Once when retired I was cruising in the Far East onboard a Norwegian ship. The captain had invited my wife and I to dinner together with other distinguished guests. Before the captain joined us at the table, his social hostess instructed us to stand as the captain approached the table).

We had our little social problems onboard. I was president of the mess at a time when during the North Atlantic passenger run that, was Liverpool to Montreal via Glasgow and Quebec the female officers were ignored socially by most of the younger officers.

During the passenger run there were endless numbers of young ladies emigrating and became very much involved in young unattached officers hence the female ships officers were somewhat forgotten. When cruising however in those days the passengers were usually rather old to attract young officers. During the cruising season the female officers were constantly invited to the officers ward room for drinks and outings ashore not so during the North Atlantic passenger season.

The senior nursing sister asked me if our wardroom committee would allow the female officers to use the officer's wardroom. The girls did not have a wardroom of their own but we did vote to have them use ours eventually. When the head hairdresser became treasurer of the wardroom the wardroom seemed to make enough money from time to time allowing us to send presents to the patients in Southend General Hospital neither the nursing sisters, purserettes or librarians had anywhere other than their cabins to relax. They could attend a movie show only during an afternoon and of course attend morning service on Sunday.

The United States Coast Guards would have a fire and boat drill exercise before allowing the ship to sail from New York. Everyone has experienced an American trying to look efficient with a peaked cap and stern look on his face. It is another thing to see the female officers of an empress ship participating in a coast guard emergency drill and getting their high heels stuck in the bottom boards of a lifeboat whilst it is being lowered. The female yells and curses at our own ships officers trying to keep their dignity in front of the American Coast Guard were something to behold.

Unfortunately the fast development of the jet aircraft soon put ocean liners off the seas in those days. The Great White Empresses days were finished and the company developed into oil tankers and bulk carriers. The passenger ships were sold and I was transferred to the cargo ships trading up to Quebec, Montreal the Saint Lawrence Seaway, Welland Canal to the Great Lakes as far as Duluth, Chicago, and Detroit. Port Huron on Lake Huron was a favourite port because labour to work the cargo was unobtainable. The whole crew were employed to load the ship, which was usually a full cargo of bagged beans for Messrs Heinz. The officers being employed as the bosses. Everyone was paid shore rates, which were quite considerable.

During the winter months although we usually got an awful battering from storms outward and homeward we had a reasonable social life in port. Because of the ice in the St Lawrence the only port called at during the winter was St. John; News Brunswick which was usually fog bound making the approach to the port very difficult. As discharging and loading took place in the same port we were there sometimes for at least three weeks. We did eventually build a couple of ships capable of making a passage through the ice on the St Lawrence during the winter. The crew on ships employed on a regular run such as the North Atlantic usually make a considerable circle of friends ashore over the years of constant trading to a particular port.

CHAPTER EIGHT

I HAD SPENT SOME years on the North Atlantic, trading up the Great Lakes to the extent that I actually had a pilots licence for Lake Erie and Lake Ontario this saved the company many hundreds of dollars in pilotage fees. Of course nothing ever remains the same. We had just commenced singling up that is taking in our ropes prior to sailing when the bos'un asked me rather alarmingly. "Did you see the T.V. just before sailing sir. All hell has let loose in Belfast. You come from Belfast, don't you?"

"Yes I do." I replied too tired to care what was happening in Belfast. After transiting the Welland Canal the Seaway and loading part cargo in Montreal the whole ships company is usually exhausted through lack of sleep.

Once I had time to myself I tuned into the overseas service of the BBC on the radio. I was very concerned in fact dammed worried to learn that Belfast seemed to be on the verge of Civil War. As we entered the Belle Isle Strait the swell became larger which meant there must be quite a sea running in the Atlantic Ocean. It wasn't too bad our speed didn't drop of too much; I was very keen to get home. In about a week's time we would be steaming up the channel. As we entered the open sea we maintained a good speed. We made the ocean passage in eleven days from Montreal to London, which was quite good. On berthing I was first down the gangway to the telephone. "Hello love how are you"?

"Are you going to get away soon do you think. Try and get a flight which will get you home in daylight I really don't want to come out at night, you understand, I will if I have to but do try and get a daylight flight if you can."

When I arrived back onboard the marine superintendent was already onboard. Music to my ears when he said my relief will be here this evening so I should get away tomorrow at a reasonable time. The ship will pay off at 1000 tomorrow morning. Actually I was home the following afternoon to a country the tension in which one could cut with a knife. But whatever the situation it is always wonderful to meet the family again. Sheelagh always brought our kids to the airport to meet me including the dog. Tara was an Alsatian and a big one at that. She eventually became too big to handle at the airport. When my plane landed the dog always went berserk to the extent that Sheelagh couldn't control him. Nevertheless I loved to see him with the kids.

My sister and my mother-in-law lived alone and although the men in the neighbourhood put wooden barriers at the bottom of the streets to try and stop gunmen. It was nevertheless important to pay a visit to the streets each night just to make sure the old folk were ok and to make them feel safe. About forty-eight hours after I was home I had a phone call from the personnel department of the company advising me that I would be required to join a new tanker at Genoa in a couple of days time. I told them when they insisted I do a tanker course at the Maritime University of Warsash. Come hell or high water you will not get me up the gangway of any more tankers. I had completed my cadetship on tankers and that was enough for any human. Besides anyway I did not have any leave last time the ship was in London and now I wanted all the leave due to me in view of the political situation in Northern Ireland so that I might have as much time with my family as possible. Well said personnel; sorry as we are about the situation in Northern Ireland our job is to Mann a fleet of ships not to get concerned with the politics of Northern Ireland. Words then got out of hand. I suggested that they also had a responsibility towards the welfare of their officers. Next day I was given an ultimatum, as there was no national emergency I refused to accept the ultimatum and that most unfortunately was my days with Canadian Pacific Steamship ended.

What was I going to do now was the question upper most in my mind. I came to the decision enjoy a well earned leave as far as one may under the present conditions prevailing at that time in the Province. Driving to Belfast each evening at 2100 through numerous army roadblocks to ensure that my sister and mother-in-law were safe. Time was marching on and getting towards when I would have to find employment. I received a phone call from a little coasting company who offered me a temporary job as master until I found something more to my liking. After a few weeks I was offered the job as marine superintendent. It was the strangest position as marine superintendent in the maritime world I ever came across.

After some months with the company. The chairman asked me to step into his office one morning. He looked at me and said. "Let's be honest with each other, shall we."

"You are after my job or at the very least a job in the industry larger than the one you now have would that be right?" "Well" said I.

"Put like that I would say your quite right." He opened the draw, put his hand in lifted out a wad of notes and handed them to me. Here he said.

"Take that and get yourself something to your liking, because we are really wasting each others time." I took the money didn't bother to count it, pushed it in my pocket. Shook hands with the man, thanked him and left. Thought to myself as I drove home, what a funny little company.

Now what shall I do. Start my own business but what? I made a decision the only thing I could do straight away with out a lot of capital was marine surveying. Next day I got a number of little business cards printed. Took myself of round all the insurance companies, shipping agents knocking on their doors etc touting for business as a draft surveyor or cargo surveyor. I must say I was very well received and soon had more offers of surveys than I could handle on my own. My very first was a cargo of onions, which arrived from the Mediterranean the worst of wear. The next was the shipment of hides from Belfast to the port of Le Havre, France the problem was the shippers and the shipping line wanted them checked from the slaughterhouse store. What a place and the stink, it all reminded me of my days loading wet hides in East Africa. I saw some of the young men who handled the hides in the place going to the loo. I too wanted to go to the loo. When I saw the loo I refused to use it. Off I went to the office, walked in and this women looking rather like a Sunday school teacher blocked my passage. Madam said I. "I want the loo and I want it now. Where is the management loo"?

"You can't use it." She replied with some venom in her voice. "You will have to ask Mr Whatever his name was." Pointing out to the yard she said.

"There is toilet out there for the workers." I looked at her and in my best bridge voice told her. "I will not use such a pig sty not even to crap in."

At that some wee baldy bespeckled guy appeared from an office wanting to know what all the fuss was about. I soon enlightened him where upon he handed me the keys of the management toilets. He looked me up and down handed me the keys and said that is were they are kept nodding in the direction of a keyboard.

Next I was called to a dispute onboard a large German cargo boat, which was discharging in Londonderry inward from the USA with a cargo Soybeans from Milwaukee. The receivers of the cargo alleged the cargo to be short. The lawyers for the cargo receivers were onboard when I got there, as indeed were the lawyers for the ship. The lawyers for the cargo employed me. When I gave my card to the ships captain and a card to the lawyers for the ship. The ships lawyers insisted that the captain should not speak to me. I was on the side of the cargo owners. The captain got most annoyed with them. He insisted that we were both seamen and through the brotherhood of the sea could only assist each other. Now it was getting embarrassing for me because he was quite wrong. I tried to explain to him that I must carry-out the instructions of my principals. He was having nothing of this I was a seaman and must help him. I ended up talking like a Philadelphian lawyer to settle everyone down.

My next assignment was technical adviser to counsel for the next of kin at the investigation into the loss of the "mv Lairdsfield". The ship had left Middlesborough bound for Haulbowline and Cork with a cargo of large steel tubes and steel plates. The plates were stowed on top of the tubes with the result the ship had no stability. The righting moment was less than her turning moment with the result, when she cleared the fairway at Middlesborough and turned south to go down the North Sea she capsized and was lost with all hands. The case lasted for eight weeks in the High Court at Middlesborough and a further two weeks in London. The solicitors in Belfast had appointed me as technical adviser to counsel for the chief officer but at the court in Middlesborough I found myself assisting I think all the counsellors for all the ships officers.

It was when carrying out a survey in a large linen company I was asked advise on shipping handkerchiefs to the Azores. This company sent the handkerchiefs they made all the way to the Azores to have them hemmed before distribution to their customers throughout the world. I decided to investigate further just how the exports of Northern Ireland are shipped to world markets. With the onset of containerisation and the development of international road transport great changes were taking place in the world of transport.

Another friend joined me in starting a Freight Forwarding company, which we called International Shipping Services Ltd. previous to that I had been working entirely alone. We had the use of a warehouse were we consolidated small consignments of cargo to make up larger container loads, dispatched them to London for further distribution throughout

Europe in TIR Groupage loads. It was possible to ship small loads to Paris in forty- eight hours much faster than the local cargo boat could get the freight to Le Havre for unforwarding to Paris. It was possible to deliver cargo to Basle in three days by the same method. Eventually we managed to ship cargo overland to the Middle East namely Teheran in days rather than weeks by sea. By this time my colleague and I decided we should have a company logo. A task given to my wife who rose to the occasion admirably. She designed 'a large Sea Eagle clasping a Compass Rose in its talons.' We used it on all our vehicles, ships and documentation.'

The above method of shipping cargo from Northern Ireland although very much faster and legally safer when comparing CMR (Convention Merchandises Routiers) The International Carriage of Goods by Road with the carriage of Goods by Sea Act. It was nevertheless very difficult to sell the idea to the local exporters. Together with the assistance of an interested professor from Queens University, Belfast. I organised a seminar at Queens University to educate business and the local legal profession on the advantages of CMR.

Upon our entry into the Common Market we obtained a number of large vehicles by leasing and by contract hirer suitable for continental work. These were vehicles with large belly tanks and sleeping accommodation in the cab. It became imperative to obtain Common Market Licences to operate such vehicles across European borders. As our application for such licences fell on deaf ears I took myself off to Brussels to visit a friend the Northern Ireland representative to Brussels to ask him to use his good offices to obtain the necessary licences. We did eventually by this time manage to obtain 25 French Licences and 20 German Licences, which gave us reasonable operational scope in Europe. Even though our business was doing very well I just could not get really interested in Road Transport. It was ships and cargoes that I found fascinating.

Our chance to get experience in the charter market presented it's self when a local scrap iron merchant asked if we might be able to help him obtain a suitable ship for his business. His regular charterer was unable to help him at this particular time. At the same time the local salt exporter assured us of a share of his salt cargoes, as he did not believe in keeping his business for one charterer. Also we had the offer of slag cargoes. My colleague an ex-chief officer from the Ben Line was rather like myself more interested in ships than vehicles. We decided to take a little German coaster on time charter. The ship was fixed on a Coastwise Charter Party at ninety-pounds per day.

Page 2

Shipper		**LINER BILL OF LADING**	B/L No.
		Reference No.	

POTTS LINE LTD.

U.K. GENERAL AGENTS:

INTERNATIONAL SHIPPING SERVICES LTD.
LONDON

Tel. 01-593-4734   Telex 897830

Consignee			
Notify address			
Pre-carriage by*	Place of receipt by pre-carrier*		
Vessel	Port of loading		
Port of discharge	Place of delivery by one-carrier*		
Marks and Nos.	Number of kind of packages; description of goods	Gross weight	Measurement

Particulars furnished by the Merchant

Freight details, charges etc.		

SHIPPED on board in apparent good order and condition, weight, measure, marks, numbers, quality, contents and value unknown, for carriage to the Port of Discharge or so near thereunto as the Vessel may safely get and lie always afloat, to be delivered in the like good order and condition at the aforesaid Port unto Consignees or their Assigns, they paying freight as indicated to the left plus other charges incurred in accordance with the provisions contained in this Bill of Lading. In accepting this Bill of Lading the Merchant expressly accepts and agrees to all its stipulations on both pages, whether written, printed, stamped or otherwise incorporated, as fully as if they were all signed by the Merchant.
Carrier not to be responsible for quality or quantity of contents, nor for description of packages, same not having been examined. If in addition to the number, particulars concerning the weight have been furnished, this Bill of Lading only constitutes a presumption as to number not as to weight loaded. In such case the weight is always presumed to be unknown. Weight also unknown if cargo has been received unweighed, the carrier having no means to check Merchants weight declaration, especially bulk cargo.
Carrier or agents not responsible for pilferage nor for damage or loss on account of frail packages and/or insufficient protection of contents.
One original Bill of Lading must be surrendered duly endorsed in exchange for the goods or delivery order.
IN WITNESS whereof the Master of the said Vessel has signed the number of original Bills of Lading stated below, all of this tenor and date, one of which being accomplished, the others to stand void.

	Freight payable at	Place and date of issue
*Applicable only when document used as a Through Bill of Lading		
	Number of original Bs/L	Signature

CHAPTER NINE

When she berthed at the Queens quay to commence loading I felt quite pleased, the first ship for our own account. She was cleared inwards from foreign on the Monday morning and sailed that afternoon for Ardrossan with five hundred tons of scrap. She was back at the Salt wharf on Wednesday sailed again late Wednesday afternoon. She operated very well and we were quite pleased with the results. Unfortunately there was a major breakdown of the machinery in the salt mine, which gave us a headache for a little while, but we survived.

A rather mean spirited shipping agent in Belfast wrote to me expressing his displeasure with me for coming from Carrickfergus were I lived to clear tonnage in the Port of Belfast. He assured me that none of the shipping agents in Belfast would countenance such action in the future. Of course it slipped his memory that he often cleared ships in Carrickfergus. I never experienced such a mean attitude from any of the other agents in Belfast but then I suppose I never became involved sufficiently with any of them to cause them concern.

We had not reached the stage yet of obtaining

decent offices for all intents and purposes my dining room at home was the office, which does not augur well if one wishes to put on a good face to the public of a business going well. The German owners of our chartered ship rang the house thinking they were in contact with a business premise. My wife answered the phone with my baby son crying around her feet to the extent she couldn't hear what the people in Hamburg were saying. She just lifted the pictures, which were hanging on the wall and gave them to junior to play with. That kept him amused and no ackward questions asked from the other end of the line. By conducting our business from home as long as possible administration costs were kept to a minimum during our formative days. Eventually we had to move to Belfast and open offices there due largely to the number of people calling at the offices for various reasons. Also we had just been awarded a contract to superintend the fabric preservation of two large bulk-carriers for Norwegian owners building at Harland & Wolff shipyard. The contract also entailed the shipment of all the paint from England to Belfast for the ships. This was an excellent contract for a young company like ours. Though working in Belfast at that time did have its problems. On a Saturday afternoon I had a phone call from one of my staff who happened to be in town shopping in High Street where our office was situated. A bomb had exploded in a funeral hearse as it passed our office. Considerable damage to the surrounding buildings took place including the breaking of all our office windows. My son and I spent Saturday afternoon obtaining hardboard. Fitting and nailing it to the window frames in an attempt to make the offices weather tight for the weekend.

At this time I had been invited by the British Overseas Trade Board to lecture two evenings per week to students attending the Belfast College of Technology studying for the Institute of Exporters Examinations. This also entailed submitting questions to the examination board for inclusion in the examination papers and marking exam papers. This proved an exhausting task sometimes especially trying to decipher some of the student's handwriting especially when trying to be fair marking examination papers.

The Department of Posts and Telegraphs in the Southern Irish Government were about to extend the telegraph service through the west coast of Ireland this entailed shipping from Scandinavia to Ireland one hundred thousand telegraph poles. We had been given to understand that the total number of poles had never been lifted from the Baltic in one year as required. Hence the contract was put out to tender and we won it. My colleague and I travelled down to Dublin to advise the department as to just how we intended to carry it out.

Having had considerable experience as chief officers planning the carriage of cargoes over many years we felt confident that we could do it. Even though the previous carrier had had the contract to himself for many years. We were given to understand that the poles had never been lifted all in one year. There was always many left over on the dockside through the winter, which meant many, were shipped in a very wet condition the following season. It was, we understood one of the largest timber contracts ever placed by an importer in Ireland. About this time I formed a shipping company which I called 'Potts line' to concentrate on shipping rather than road transport. The 'Potts Line' became part of the 'International Shipping Company'

We that is 'Potts Line' chartered two ships each with a large single hatch and slings fitted. All the cargo would be sling fitted which speeded up the loading and discharge of the cargo considerably. It was a condition of the charter-party that the ships would be sling fitted and that the ships officers would be responsible for the cargo being so shipped and that the ships crew would secure the cargo. Most of the cargo was shipped to Limerick and the remainder to Dublin largely from Finland. One of our ships ran into severe weather coming through the Pentland Firth, which played havoc with the deck cargo. When the ship arrived in Dublin the cargo was sticking out over the side making it very difficult to berth the ship. The Dockers refused to handle the cargo. I jumped into the car and in a few hours was in Dublin talking to the Dockers. It was made clear to them they were not dealing with some big international company but a couple of sailors trying to establish a shipping company here in Ireland. I thought the Dockers were a good bunch of guys who tried very much to help us. We expressed our gratitude to them by taking them up to the pub. Having a few jars together and passing a few bob over the table and everyone was happy. The ship was discharged in record time and away she sailed.

Once whilst one of our ships was loading in Finland a dispute developed between the ships officers and the stevedores over the quantity of poles, which had been loaded. I needed to get to a telex machine to send my instructions in writing which the ships captain had asked for. An easy request to most shipping companies except at that time which was about 2200 in Belfast a gun battle had broken out between the army and the IRA. This just practically at my office door.

The army refused passage to the container yard in which my office was situated. My oldest son was with me as a sort of escort which was very necessary around Belfast late at night in those troubled times. After much talking to the senior officer in command of the situation. I told him.

"These gunmen are effecting the situation of ships loading in Finland. It is not just what you see going on in the street here. Do you want these guys to have that much influence"?

"Ok you can get to your office but do try and work without the lights if you can, use a torch." Which luckily we had one in the car. It was a very uncomfortable situation to be in and at the same time keep up communications with a ship loading at Toppila in Finland and give clear instructions to the ship. However we managed to sort out the situation and get the ship away.

One morning during normal office hours a soldier from the parachute regiment came into the office and told us to evacuate the premises. Apparently there was a bomb in the office next door, as he was advising us why we had to evacuate the bomb went off blowing all the windows in. The girls had their hair covered with broken glass and flames seemed to be sweeping across the windows. We all managed to get safely down the stairs and into the street which was covered, with porn magazines. The shop across the street from us, a paper shop also stocked girlie magazines, which was badly damaged in the blast. If girls ever deserved a medal. The office girls of Belfast in those days certainly did. They deserved much credit for remaining at their various offices and workstations throughout the troubles.

On a Saturday night I had gone out with a few friends for a drink when the barmaid called me to the phone. My wife was on to tell me the police had rang to say the office had been bombed. I drove to the Governor Road but the police had the whole area cordoned of. A bomb attacked had taken place against the business premises in the area and now a gun battle was raging. Approaching the area was out of the question best wait until Sunday morning. On Sunday morning I arrived to find the offices totally destroyed and everything in them. The staff who were of mixed religions were all there of their own volition trying to clear some of the mess up and salvage what they could. On Monday we commenced work again as usual in our bombed out offices. This was the seventh time we had suffered severe bomb damage to our premises in High Street and the Governor Road. One could be forgiven for going back to sea and forgetting about trying to run a business ashore. It was the effort and tenacity displayed by the staff, which made me, feel. Keep at it; don't give in to terrorists.

Before our ships called at Toppila I travelled there to talk to the agents and stevedores about the contract etc. I was met coming of the plane by one of the locals in typical Laplander gear. The first thought entered my head was, here no one would know about Belfast and its troubles. At least my head will get peace. First thing the taxi driver said to me was. "Where are you from sir?"

Naturally I said Belfast he immediately replied. "Oh boom, boom, plenty trouble."

I immediately thought, my god can one not escape from it all for just a little while. Then I thought don't be so bloody selfish your away from the real trouble for a week or so, the staff aren't, they are still dodging bomb scares, riots and nightly gun battles. Some of the things people say makes one think just were do people get their information from. It must be their local media taking leave of their senses.

The local agent at Toppila was also one of the local doctors, which I found to be a turn up for the books. A doctor running after ships. I told her so but she found it wonderful to be able to meet so many interesting foreigners in such a remote place as Northern Finland. Over dinner trying to keep clear of the subject of politics I couldn't help remarking that I get the feeling. "Whilst I recognize that Finland is not part of the communist bloc nevertheless people seem to have, if not a fear of Russia, certainly a healthy respect for Russia".

She tacitly agreed. I felt I was perhaps sailing close to the wind with my remarks so I didn't pursue the subject.

On completion of my business I returned to Helsinki. Later I decided I would complete my business in southern Finland by calling at Kotka and Hamina instead of returning in a few months time. From Kotka my agent arranged for a car to take me to Hamina the driver of which spoke little English. It was dark when we left Kotka and being Finland in the autumn the ground was covered in snow. The road seemed to be just a long strait narrow passage through an endless forest of coniferous trees. It was so dark with just the moon and the stars for light. It seemed almost as if one could reach up and touch them. All we needed now was to be chased by wolves to make the atmosphere turn to real 'boys own' stuff. I found the whole car trip very eerie indeed.

On arrival home in Belfast I was invited by Lord Mellchet who was Minister for Education in Northern Ireland to take a seat on the Northern Ireland Education Advisory Council and the GCE Examination Board. I did explain to the Board that I travelled quite a lot and that I had not attended University. They in turn made it clear to me that they had enough people with university degrees but none with the experience of the world and the vocational education I had. They were keen that I should take the seat so of course I did. However I was most unhappy about the Official Secrets Act and many aspects of the Council. After about two years I knew I would have to leave otherwise I might land myself in trouble. Obviously the thing to do was to resign and this I did.

Our vehicles were now making trips to Iran on a regular basis. Business in the Middle East was booming to the extent that the ports in the Persian Gulf just could not handle the amount of cargo arriving at the Gulf Ports. Congestion was becoming serious and more and more vehicles from Europe were making the journey by road to the Middle East. Which was causing it's own problems. The Germans were not issuing sufficient licences for TIR vehicles to cross Germany thus causing more and more vehicles to use the German Railway kangaroo system. Soon this system could not cope with the traffic and special trailers were needed to pass under the low bridges on the German rail network. As though that wasn't enough the Turkish roads couldn't really cope either with the traffic on their roads. The roads were never built to take such large numbers of heavy forty-foot vehicles. Crossing frontiers was becoming a headache; sometimes the customs were reasonable other times they were beyond reason. I could see serious trouble coming from some quarter before long.

A couple of days after arriving from Finland I was off to the Middle East. My wife remarked. "You wouldn't have moved so fast for a shipping company. Different when it's your own, isn't it she said"? That made me think I'm spending nearly as much time away from home as I did when I was sea.

POTTS LINE chartered vessel *ILKA* from HAMINA
Discharging Telegraph Poles at Dublin:
Note: Logo on the funnel

CHAPTER TEN

My idea was to find a berth with about nineteen feet of water at all states of the tide. Charter a 2500 to 3000 dwt vessels and get into berths the bigger ships couldn't. Why hasn't someone else done so? I went to the Emirates travelled from Ras al Khaimah all along the coasts searching around Dubai, Abu Dhabi and Sarjah. The only berth with twenty feet of water enough to let a 2500 to 3000 dwt alongside and exclude large ships was that being used by the rulers yacht. Somehow I felt His Majesty would not take lightly to my idea that he should anchor his yacht of the berth and give Potts Line the use of it. I gleaned much information about the area, which I was able to put to good use at a later date. Whilst I didn't get just what I went out east for I did put my newfound knowledge to good use. I did end up with a contract to ship all the bricks from Belfast to Dubai for the building of the new barracks for the Dubai Defence Force.

A large well known Shipbroking Company 'with whom we had shipped many LCL loads to Portugal' themselves well established in London. Were very keen to set up a freight forwarding company in the

Home Counties. I was keen to become a member of the Baltic Exchange. Having asked, they very kindly agreed to assist us obtain shares in the Baltic Exchange which was a prerequisite to becoming a member. In consideration of their kind assistance we in turn would help them establish a freight forwarding company in the midlands. We agreed mutually to assist each other fulfil our ambitions. Another large liner company with whom we had considerable dealings agreed to second our application for membership.

I think the first thing to do was to understand the exchange. To be a member it was necessary to hold shares in the exchange and to be represented on the floor of the exchange by your broker or agent. A principle cannot trade on the floor. As both our companies were in fact principles in the manner in which they traded it became necessary to have a company to act as an agents only. To accommodate the foregoing the company "International Navigation Services" was formed which accommodated our trading on the floor. I engaged a very active young Greek broker to join International Navigation Services as the company representative on the floor of the exchange. The International Navigation Services became part of the International Shipping Services group of companies.

I had by this time commenced a liner service run by 'Potts Line' from Antwerp and Rotterdam on the continent and Avonmouth to Piraeus, Istanbul and Alexandria with inducement this service went very well indeed. We had been offered a full cargo of fertilizer from Alexandria to Marseilles the freight rate was such that it was hard not to show some interest in it. Westbound cargo paying a decent freight rate was always difficult to come across in the Mediterranean. We had had a fair share of the fruit cargoes, which the conference lines had not lifted for one reason or another. Our broking company went ahead and fixed the cargo for us on one of our time-chartered ships.

It was about this time when I was going away with my family on holidays to Cavetat in Yugoslavia. My colleague ran the family and I up to the airport to get our plane. I had said to him I am not going to disclose just were we would be holidaying because I always received calls of some description regarding the business and this time I really didn't want any of that. However I did renege, before saying good-bye I did advise my fellow directors exactly were I was going to holiday. Whilst sitting by the swimming pool of the hotel a steward advised me that there was a message in the foyer of the hotel for me. Up I went to the foyer to receive a telex a mile long. Just looking at the length of the message led me to swear. "My god what has happened now?" The sum total was the ship bound from Alexandria to Marseilles was in difficulty. The master believed the cargo to be on fire. There appeared to be smoke emantating from the cargo holds through the hold vents. It was the master's intention to put into Leghorn as a port of refuge and there declare General Average. I suggested to our office to be careful about participating in average just now. It was most important for us that the master knew he was in peril and not just thought he was in peril. The owners had invited us as time charters to join them in average. I had advised our office to just wait a little to the situation clarifies itself.

Upon arrival at Leghorn it was discovered that the ship was not on fire but that the cargo was given off pungent fumes. From a seaworthy point of view the ship was not in peril in anyway. She was eventually cleared from Leghorn to continue her voyage to Marseilles. Upon arrival at Marseilles it was discovered that the cargos physical and chemical composition had changed causing the fumes during the voyage. It was further discovered that the hold ceiling on the tank tops had become damaged by the change in the chemical and physical composition of the cargo. Big trouble was obviously brewing. To date the owners had acted as real gentlemen, being most understanding and considerate throughout. I had by this time arrived home from my holidays. We had a meeting in Marseilles with all interested parties in the situation. During the discussion the cargo owners seemed to be somewhat disturbed by the fact that my co-director and I were from that awful boom- boom town Belfast. For what reason I cannot say, maybe it was my imagination but they were not too happy.

The truth all started to emerge now. The cargo had been shipped to Alexandria as fertilizer. Whilst on the quay at Alexandria the cargo had been on fire. It had been extinguished and much of the cargo had been re-bagged for shipment back to Marseilles. This knowledge we were not privy to when we loaded the cargo in Alexandria. The owners insisted that we complete the time charter-party, which we really wanted to do. It was in our interests to keep the ship. The receivers and owners of the cargo wanted the whole sorry mess dealt with as expediently and quietly as possible as we all did. I wanted a bond lodged in our bank to which we and the receivers of the cargo were signatories, covering all our expenses including the time charter costs. This they were more than willing to do eventually we got everything sorted to our entire satisfaction.

Upon arrival in Belfast I couldn't help wondering what would be next but it was good to have another problem settled. One of the difficulties running a shipping company with all chartered ships in the period I am writing about is. Notwithstanding the fact that all our ships were entered at Lloyds against Charteres' Liabilities. It is not the same as having the support of a P&I Club. All owners have their Protection and Indemnity Club, which of course one pays for the services of their own club in the form of an insurance premium. Each year the club will have 'calls' that is, each member will top up the clubs reserves as deemed necessary by the committee of the club. If an owner has ships entered in his club then most clubs will allow that owner to enter his chartered ships. Not owning ships we were not members of a P&I club hence we could not enter any ships in a club. Therefore I attended to all our P&I work myself. Often a time charter-party will be claused as follows: 'Charterers to have the benefit of the owners P&I Club as far as the rules permit.' All our time charters contained such a clause, though the benefit of such a clause to a charterer is often very limited. For the aforementioned reason running "Potts Line" was very demanding. Very considerable thought was required with every move and action taken. Especially in the maritime world, bearing in mind the world to day is very litigious conscience and the legal profession do not come cheaply.

It was whilst reading Maritime Law at the Belfast College of Technology when studying for Part "A" Extra Master that the position of a master was brought home to us poverty stricken students. One of our legal textbooks explained in a famous case in tort. A passenger had sustained an injury whilst using the accommodation ladder on a passenger ship in the port of Genoa. The passenger took an action against the captain, and the bos'un of the ship. The owner had immunity in tort under the contract of carriage in the passage ticket, which did not extend to the servants of the owner. It was suggested by the author, that had it been possible the passenger would have been better advised to take the action against the shipowner. A more substantial defendant if one was to win their case. Apart from who had the duty of care the writer suggested that masters are "poor and simple folk" We students took great exception at being referred to as poor and simple folk. Having now experienced much more of the commercial world I can only say that truer words were never written about shipmasters.

One of our ships had berthed in Istanbul during the first day of discharging some of the cargo had been taken away for sampling by the customs and the receivers. Needless to say with the luck of the Potts Line the receivers refused to accept the cargo hence all discharging was stopped. The cargo had been loaded in Antwerp as edible fat in large cans but the sample showed the edible fat to be edible oil. Lucky for us the cargo had been sold on a CIF basis and we had been paid the freight. The port authorities insisted that the ship be moved from the discharging berth to a lay by berth until the receivers were prepared to resume taking delivery of the cargo.

My colleague was standing by the telex machine when this rather long message came in over the teletext. I watched him as his face turned white and he looked pale.

"What is the problem?

You look like you have seen a ghost".

"There is a message from some Insurance Company in Genoa when you read it, you'll do more that see ghosts. I suggest you take it down to the loo to read it. They're suing us for the equivalent of the reserves of the World Bank in dollars. The cargo in Istanbul, the receivers are alleging that it is not what is declared on the Bill of Lading and they are holding us responsible."

"That's good," said I.

"If they had been looking for a few thousand dollars I would have been very worried but they're not they are looking for the impossible. We can't do it so why worry, we just can't. That is standard practise for any insurance company to try and cover their losses. They'll be suing everybody on Gods earth by now. Have a cup of tea man you'll get over it. We will just have to rely on our Demise Clause in the Bills of Lading and no doubt the owners' P&I Club will rely on the Merchants' Special Responsibilities Clause. I must confess though I am pleased the ship is flying the Romanian Flag. Our agent seems rather happier about that also. Believe me, there will be much wealing and dealing going on out there just now but it will not affect us substantially, I hope. Just make sure that we give the owners P&I Club maximum support. It may well require one of us taking ourselves out to Istanbul for a couple of days. I suggest you contact our agent and make arrangement to do just that. Get him to book you into the Hilton, you'll like that. I can recommend it especially the London bar down stairs. Anyway it would be a very poor show on our part if none of the directors takes some interest in the problem and furthermore is seen to do so".

I told my wife Sheelagh that I would have to make a trip to Istanbul she suggested that if I let her have my discharge book she could fill it in as one does when joining and leaving a ship. I'm away now nearly as much as I was when I was sea. At least when at sea I was guaranteed leave. Now it seems I come home, run round the table and run back up to the airport. Myself and another director travelled to Istanbul. After a long and somewhat tiring meeting it was agreed the best solution was to leave everything in the hands of the owners' P & I Club. This we did and nothing of any consequences was ever heard of the matter.

International Shipping Services vehicle loading in our London depot for Tehran

CHAPTER ELEVEN

Due to the congestion at Persian Gulf ports as mentioned else where in this book an inordinate number of TIR vehicles were passing through Turkey to and from the Gulf. The roads in Turkey were suffering wear and tear, which they were never expected to. Without notice the Turkish government levied a special road tax on international vehicles transiting the country. Unfortunately the contracts we had for the carriage of cargo to and from Teheran did not have a force majeure clause in them, which was an awful omission on our part. Contractually we were in a very difficult situation because we just could not afford to carry the cargo without getting some contribution towards the extra costs incurred in the form of the Turkish tax.

I suggested to the shippers and the consignees' of the cargo that they might make some contribution towards the costs incurred by us. All international road transport companies were in the same position as we were. Therefore they could either fly the cargo to Teheran our engage another carrier. Should we renege on the contract? Threats of moving to litigation by the shipper would solve nothing for anyone. It most certainly would have no bearing on any action I might take. Eventually the problem was solved by subcontracting the whole contract to a very large Eastern Block Carrier who was more interested in hard currency than the actual rate charged for the job, within reason that is. We also earned a little more in the form of commission. Everyone was happy in the end.

Just after solving one mess and sitting by my office desk, with my mind on the beach in Barbados and other things. The phone rang, my secretary answered it. Mr Ryan for you. Hello Mr Ryan what can I do for you? In a very hesitant voice he asked me how I was and then as if something was terribly wrong by the tone of his voice he said.

"Are you busy, I would like to chat with you sometime. Would you come out and see me?" "Sure I will, how about now? Ok, I'm on my way," said I.

When I arrived his secretary showed me into his office. As he got up from his desk to shake hands and welcome me. He looked decidedly nervous. Good to see you Bill, what's your problem? He said not really a problem, and then there was a hell of a long silence. He started talking about the weather at length; I wondered what all this was about. Then he said. "You carry a lot of our products, how would you like to carry it all"?

I didn't answer I felt there was more to come. He said to me just then. "You know I do most of the work here. It is I who does the buying and the shipping." Said I, "A lot of responsibility."

"Yes but I don't get the recognition for it that I should get." Then the bomb went off.

"If I gave you all our freight to carry? Would you give me about 3% of the freight you earn from us"?

I was a little taken aback.

"Bill, I know how you must feel and I know it must be most embarrassing for you to put such a proposition to me. Now I want you to do something for me."

"Sure anything you want," he said.

"Please, forget this conversation ever took place, just forget I was in your office to day, 'back handers' are just not my scene." That was the end of the conversation.

On the drive back to my office I couldn't help thinking of another similar episode in England this time. A large multi-national who had a lot of freight coming out of Northern Ireland being shipped to various parts of the world. This cargo was all controlled from the company's head office in England by their shipping manager. I and one of my directors had a meeting with this individual in England which was pre arranged. We had travelled to England especially to meet him. The idea was to get more of his cargo allocated to our services. Considering what this guy controlled being exported from Northern Ireland our share of his cargoes was miniscule.

After dinner we all naturally went to the loo and as I was washing my hands he was doing likewise beside me he said.

"Yes I can arrange for your company to increase your share of our freight. It will cost you." He lowered his voice and suggested we leave a little car with the keys in it on the waste ground at the back of the hotel here I just said.

"I'll talk it over with my colleague here and let you know."

The shipping manager just took his leave of us and as we shook hands he just said.

We'll be in touch."

Needless to say we never did bother to get in touch with him. To me the guy was just a bum.

The company employed two young ladies as freight canvassers, one in the North and one in the South of Ireland. Should any of these young ladies need support in dealing with a client one of the directors would accompany her on a visit to the firm. A particular firm always said to our canvasser we are far too expensive to deal with. What they didn't know was that the freight forwarder they gave all their freight to gave it all to a particular carrier who in turn carried his freight to England for on forwarding to it's destination by an English carrier. We would have carried it direct to the continent for him, which was bound to be much cheaper. Obviously some body was getting their palm greased because all these guys had to be paid. Their charges must be on top of what our freight charges were as final carriers. Our freight rates must have been cheaper.

Just as I walked through the office door the phone rang. A call from International Shipping Service's Bank. I took the call the manager wanted to have a 'wee yarn with me' as he put it. "Ok, lets fix a time and a date," said I.

"Tomorrow morning 1030. Good see you then."

As I drove home that evening thinking of my meeting in the morning with the bank manager. A patrol of commandos was walking along the footpath on either side of the street. Suddenly there was a rattle of machine gun fire; I could see the bullets strike the railings of a building on the other side of the street as I approached it. I jammed the brakes on very quickly indeed. As I stopped the car behind me pulled out round me. An elderly couple were sitting in the front. The old guy who was driving looked at me as though I had crawled out from under a sod. Needless to say the old edjit hadn't realized just why I had stopped. The occupants of both our cars came very close to meeting their maker. I noticed one of the soldiers lying in a protective mode on a little girl. When there seemed to be a lull in the shooting I revved the engine and made myself scarce.

It had never been my intention to be a businessman. I only became involved in business as a means of being with my family at a time I believed them to be in danger due to the troubles in Northern Ireland. To-date we had had our offices bombed seven times. If not as the direct target then at least next to it.

I arrived home somewhat annoyed. Quite frankly I was thinking more about why the bank should ring the office wanting to talk to me personally, they had never done that before. My wife took one look at me and asked

"What's bugging you"? I told her about being caught between the army and a terrorist's gun battle. She just remarked.

"That was not the best of areas you were travelling through."

"No, but that is life to-day in our fair city" I mumbled as I hung my coat up.

Next morning in the bank the atmosphere was very relaxed more that I expected.

"Ralph come in, come in, I hope you don't mind me asking you to come in for a little chat." "Of course not" said I.

The truth of the matter was I was very concerned I knew there was a rabbit away somewhere. Bank managers don't just call a customer in to their office just for fun. It soon came to the surface.

"We had your financial director pay us a visit when you were away. You seem to be travelling quite a lot now."

"Yes indeed I do."

He applied for a loan on behalf of the company usually your signature would be on any such application, such an application would have been via the board. At this stage it would be harmful for me to deny knowledge of the application. I did know that International Shipping was experiencing an awful cash flow problem.

The main problem was caused through our propensity to obtain a loan instead of suing our debtors for our outstanding debts. To move to litigation too quickly usually means the end of any business relationship. The greatest problem was the fact that most of our debtors were on the continent not just round the corner were one could have a cosy chat and get some money from your client.

Another problem was a shipper would give you some cargo but once you expected to be paid they would give the next shipment to your competitor. To make matters worse they would pay your statements on the drip feed. In other words they would never pay a statement off in full, just a little at a time. In actual fact you were financing their business. That was life in business throughout the world at that time it had little if anything to do with the political situation in Northern Ireland. In so far as one could, one had to learn to live with such a situation in the groupage and full load international road transport business. The world of ocean freight and bills of lading, charter- parties etc. was all very different. It had tradition and long established historical rules upon which it had been established through the centuries. The men who ran old well established shipping companies were in themselves men of integrity. Though they were men who understood the old maxim of 'Joint Venture' hence when they came together and tried 'something' they were not considered by their peers to be 'wide boys.'

During my few years in business I knew I needed a bit more knowledge about the business world than what I might glean from my studies of shipmasters business. I enrolled in a course run jointly by the Irish Institute of Management and the Department of Business Studies of Queens University Belfast. The course was called Higher Finance for the Senior Business Executive it was residential and held at the Bohill Auto Inn, Coleraine from Friday night until Monday morning every weekend for six months. Lectures commenced immediately upon arrival and lasted each day until late into the night. I knew during that course I had brought the International Shipping Group of companies to far in such a short time. As a group of companies we did not have a strong financial base far from it. I started the company off with only £50 a hole in my shoe and the moral support of my brother and the faith of my wife, Sheelagh. As I stood in the office of the bank manager that morning I could feel the 'cookies coming home to roost.'

The phone rang, as the manager slowly picked up the phone to answer it, I started to become somewhat philosophical. I thought if we do go under, terrible as it might be but only a lot of people will loose jobs. I thought in those few moments as the manager answered his phone of the wild nights in the North Atlantic and the Arctic when we wondered if we would see the morning. In those few minutes I put my world into perspective. The manager's voice brought me to my senses.

"Ralph I very much regret to say to you, but the bank is very concern that, as far as we can observe If anything should happen to you we would not be willing to continue to support the company as it is presently constructed."

I stood up shook hands with the man and I just looked him in the eye and said.

"I read your signal" and left. As I walked to my office I thought to myself if I was in your shoes Mr Manager I would feel the exact same about our organisation.

I always felt during a board meeting that when I put an idea on the table it was usually accepted without too much debate. That is bad and I knew it. I also knew I had been unwell and was not sleeping. The doctor had put me on Valium, just a couple at night he suggested. The time had now come when I was taking them like 'smarties'. Thankfully the Potts Line was performing reasonably well, but a run of bad luck and it too could take a 'severe list.' One thing I certainly could not control and that was the vagaries of world trade. The trouble we had with the cargos of edible oil in Turkey is an example. Only the good Lord controls the weather and we rely on the weather so much for a voyage to be successful. I couldn't help thinking to myself that the writing was on the wall for International Shipping Services. Upon arrival back at the office I arranged for a board meeting as soon as possible.

CHAPTER TWELVE

"Good morning everyone as you all know I had a meeting with the bank yesterday at their request. It would seem they are none to happy about the recent application for funding with respect to our cash flow difficulties. We can rob Peter to pay Paul by having our shipping interests help finance our road transport. Selling some vehicles closing either London or Dublin cutting staff. One thing we can do is put real pressure on our debtors by giving them seven days notice of us moving to litigation to recover our debts. I suggest we do that immediately. The alternative is 'voluntary liquidation' to keep trading one thing you will have to do is settle that tax account. The revenue will hit us with a tax bill much quicker than you expect if some action is not taken now. The real problem is as I see it. If our debtors think we are in trouble you have no hope of getting paid. They will just sit on their creditors accounts waiting for a liquidator to try and collect them. They know it will then be months before they have to pay up. We will have a good look at our situation in depth to day. Have a sleep on it, tomorrow we'll meet again and discuss it all further. Perhaps then we could come to a solution, agreed, gentlemen.

Good you all agree."

I knew I had a personnel problem and that was I just couldn't get interested in road transport. It seemed to me to be so uninteresting if not down right boring. Shipping and seafaring was a way of life but then I would say that. I would be more than happy to sell my share of the business to my colleagues but I knew they hadn't the money. I had suggested this a few times in the past to one of our directors but the offer fell on deaf ears. Furthermore he felt he was rather old now to run a business on his own. Retirement was of more interest to him. The other director wasn't so interested as to want to become deeply involved himself in running a business.

Agreement was reached to open an office for Potts Line in the city and close the road transport offices with a view to closing International Shipping Services completely. I felt we had a responsibility towards our employees many of whom had been through some awful times in the city during the IRA attacks on business premises. There was an argument for closing the Dublin office. The amount of business we did in the south could easily be controlled from the Belfast office now that the American Export Lines was pulling out of Europe. In association with other smaller companies and through the good offices of the Chamber of Commerce I had started a pension plan for the employees. It was considered a good plan and therefore it was most important that it should be protected from the liquidators.

This idea was to take considerable planning and legal action. If we liquidated now we felt provided the liquidator could get the debts on the continent settled where the out lay was considerable, sold the vehicles, sold our EEC Transport licences together with a large new comptometer machine all of which were worth quite a lot. Our creditors should be very happy.

Our plans to go into voluntary liquidation with our road transport company were taken because it was felt that the future looked grim to say the least. Two of the largest companies in the business we learned, had to pay up front before their vehicles could board the ferries. No longer would the ferry company allow them to run a monthly account. Business in the Province was becoming very difficult indeed. In the immediate future we could only see more debt on the horizon. A few months past the police had followed one of our vehicles into our London depot threatening to summons us over the state of it's 'hanger shackles.' Our London manager was most upset because the vehicle in question was supposed to be new. The police were most emphatic this was not a new vehicle. The crap really hit the fan then. My colleagues on the board wanted to move at once to litigation against the supplier. That was going to cost more money and time proving it. It would take at least eighteen months before it would come to court. Especially the way the courts where then, they were so very busy. The company's solicitor appointed a liquidator on our behalf. After many meetings with him a creditors meeting was called in the usual legal fashion. Where upon the company moved to voluntary liquidation.

All our documents, files etc., were moved to the liquidator's offices as was everything and anything, which could be of help to him in the liquidation. Naturally the liquidation was settled in a true Belfast style. Terrorist put a bomb in the premises next door to the liquidators which exploded destroying both offices and that were the end of International Shipping Services Limited. The liquidation couldn't continue in the manner required by law. There was nothing left to continue with. The liquidator was left to do the best he could in a bad situation.

Our shipping interests continued from our new offices in the city but problems never seemed to go away. This morning we received news from Port Louis, Mauritius that a cyclone had hit the island. Our ship the *Parthenon* was delayed by the storm and at present was riding out the weather on the lee side of the land. Apparently there was considerable damage in the port therefore when the *Parthenon* would berth discharge may be slow. The services operated by Potts Line was fortnightly to the Eastern Mediterranean calling at Piraeus, Istanbul and Alexandra with inducement. The Indian Ocean service was also fortnightly to Colombo and Mauritius. Both services loaded at Avonmouth, London, Antwerp and Rotterdam. Considerable fi-

POTTS LINE Chartered vessel VICMAR
NAVIGATOR Loading Buses in London for Mauritius

nances were required to keep the services running. Together with the charter costs which was usually $2000 daily thirty days in advance. The bunkers remaining in the ship on delivery had to be paid for plus port costs.

When we purchased bunkers it was done through an international bunker broker that way we could get twenty-one days credit. Buying direct from the oil companies did not help ones cash flow. They demanded payment up front. Everything was a question of cash flow it almost consumed ones thinking. It was imperative that freight was paid on singing Bills of Lading. Often it was necessary to obtain the assistance of the bank when a ship was coming on hire. This was only for a couple of weeks until the first freights were paid which was often within a few days of commencing to load. On our liner service it was possible to have a ship loading for the Eastern Mediterranean and one loading for the Indian Ocean at the same time. We would possibly have a ship loading timber or telegraph poles in the Baltic at the same time. When freights were paid in a foreign bank it often took sometime for it to be transferred to our bank.

When our last ship was coming on hire on picking up inward pilot at Avonmouth a little help was required from the bank. This facility had been arranged or so we thought and when I contacted the bank to come and sign for it I was stunned when it was denied. A sum of only £30000 was required for a week. Notwithstanding the fact that the sum of some £100,000 of assigned freight was offered as surety almost immediately, nothing would make the bank manager honour his word. The fact that we liquidated our road transport services had given the young bank manager cause for concern if not a severe fright. Our legal advisers were most insistent that we take an action against the bank immediately for a 'breach of contract.' I refused as I felt a solution was needed now not next year. What was important was to honour our contracts of affreightment. There was considerable cargo booked at all the ports and I was determined to carry it. Furthermore I was really beginning to get totally fed up carrying the total weight of the company myself. Agreement at all times was not what was required; it was debate and understanding in full of the shipping world. Business was never my forte and I knew within myself I had built the International Shipping group of companies up too big too quickly and without daddy's cheques book or anyone else for that matter at my back

There were many people over the years that had expressed a keen interest in getting involved with us either as partners or just by putting money into the firm as an investment. I thought now is the time to contact those interested in the Line and make an offer to them. The old judge's maxim 'poor and simple folk' came home to roost. One guy who always cut a dash about town hadn't the price of an 'ice cream poke' his wife was the power in their house. I wasn't too keen to really get involved with them. The next gentleman was very keen indeed. He actually took me along to his bank with him to meet the manager. We had a great discussion but, unfortunately, he was six figures in the red and the manager made it clear to him he wouldn't lend him a 'stamp' never mind money until he did something about his present debt. The one man who may have been of some help admitted that it would be unlikely that I would be acceptable to his family politically. It took him an awful long time to come to that conclusion. I think many people like the sound of their own voice. They saw a young company start with nothing and progress very well at least it appeared so on the surface. Basically their bluff was called, even the Potts Line bank approached the company canvassing to be the lines bankers. At the end of the day they were of no help what so ever.

I approached one of our port agents who were part of a much larger shipping organisation. They understood the assignment of freights even if the bank didn't. A deal was worked out between us, the cargo was loaded the ship maintained her schedule and everyone was reasonably happy. It was obvious the bank had totally undermined our operations to the extent I had grave reservations about continuing. I knew once confidence was lost it would take years before it could be built up again within the industry. The whole operation was becoming a one-man band not by design but by the standard of senior management. Many very experienced people in the industry based in London advised me most strongly that I must get an office in London quickly and work from there. Unfortunately we had closed our London office at Dagenham when we closed down International Shipping. To recover from the damage done by the bank and build the line up again would require me to move to London to live. That I was not prepared to do not under any circumstances. Personally I felt the thing to do was to wrap the whole operation up and go back to sea.

When I discussed my plans with my wife and family my wife was delighted. She said with that old business you were away just as much. At least in the Merchant Navy you had your leave there was no leave when you were running a business the size of yours virtually single-handed. The bank stated that they wanted the overdraft paid within, I think, seven days and had served notice on the directors of International Shipping Services to that effect. If the money were not forth coming, they would move to litigation to recover it. When I suggested liquidating Potts Line the directors of the company were all for it. The demand from the bankers of International Shipping Services Ltd for the overdraft was the catalyst, which brought about swift agreement to get rid of all our business operations. The overdraft was secured by the director's guarantee, which kept the heat on our board. Anyway we were not going to jump in the manner suggested by the bank. We had the support of our legal advisers and as far as I was concerned it was going to be settled by negotiation. I had the debt reduced to £10,000 paid off by the directors on the drip feed. So the pain of settling the debt was greatly reduced.

The Potts Line was also liquidated, the bank sued the directors for the overdraft which was quite a small overdraft considering the level of our operations. There had been a case in the high courts in Dublin in which a northern bank, the defendant, had moved to litigation unfortunately for the bank the judge found for the plaintiff

Through our legal team in Belfast I was able to engage the barrister for the plaintiff on the northern bank case. Obviously a man of experience in bank cases. We met in a pub on the border and over lunch decided a plan of action. He agreed to join our team I let the bank know that it was my intention to move to litigation for 'Breach of Contract' and 'Negligence'.

A large black car drew up at my front door from which these two guys like something from a Chicago movie alighted. My wife disappeared into the garden, as these two gentlemen demanded the banks overdraft. They said, "We do not see any appearance of wealth and yet we know you are a millionaire considering the money that passed through the company of which you own the greatest shareholding." Let me tell you guys something; I don't like the cut of your jib. You both have a very threatening disposition and I don't like it so please leave. My legal team will be in touch with you very soon. At that they got up and left. At a further meeting with the bank we settled the whole case for £ 4000, which was nothing really.

The staff all received their redundancy money our oldest director took retirement my colleague found another job. Whilst looking for a job back at sea I was very lucky. Our legal team gave me a job as a temporary legal assistant. The first job I had in the courts was a 'divorce' I was rather concerned because I had all the divorce papers to deal with. I sat just below the judge handing him the legal papers in their correct order as the case proceeded. I couldn't help thinking if someone slams a door and all my papers go flying in the air with the draft, the couple may very well end up getting married in the confusion instead of divorced.

My next case was a rather nasty car accident. So long as I kept my papers in order I managed quite well in the court. Apart from arranging a mortgage on a ship I had nothing whatsoever to with shipping. My time was taken up largely with helping to prepare a case for a planning application. In the meantime a very large Japanese shipping company offered me a berth as a chief officer. I was assured after a voyage as chief officer I would be promoted to captain provided I was considered worth it and that I wished to continue in the company. The voyages were to be very long and I felt it best that under the circumstances in which I was returning to the sea I should take it easy at first. Try and do a short trip first, I had been ashore nearly nine years. During that time there had been many changes at sea. There were now great emphases on passage planning and routeing in the channel and in other congested areas. One morning I received a rather interesting large brown envelope. The contents were even more interesting it was a lovely coloured brochure about the enclosed shipping company and its ships together with a letter inviting me to come to Newcastle-Upon-Tyne for an interview. I think my wife Sheelagh was more delighted about the offer than I was. She rightly said, "You feel as though you have lost everything and perhaps you feel a bit of a social failure. If you get a nice ship on a good run you'll soon feel like a new man." She was quite right really. I had built up quite a large shipping operation from nothing and had also achieved other things. It was just rather sad to watch it all start to come adrift.

I arrived in Newcastle-Upon-Tyne and made my way to the company's office where upon I was made most welcome. They new all about my shipping company operated by a fleet of chartered ships. When they mentioned salary I must have had a strange look on my face because they immediately turned over the page of the book in front of the personnel manager and said.

"Would that salary suit you? If we like each other it would only be for a short time. We would ask you to do one voyage as chief officer and if mutually agreeably we will give you a command after that. I see your Masters' Certificate has endorsements in it for Extra

Master. Which paper do you need to finish It."?

I said "Physics" and I don't intend to finish it, I don't think there is anything to be gained by more studying at my age now."

"Yes maybe your right." he suggested.

"Surely you must think about your past achievements"?

"I try not to"?

"Well are you coming to us or not, what is it to be"?

"If the jobs mine of course I'll join you, delighted to." That was the start of a very happy seventeen years at sea again, before medical redundancy.

CHAPTER THIRTEEN

I JOINED THE MV *Washington* in Amsterdam she was a lovely ship just new from the Japanese shipyards and full of gadgets. She wasn't particularly big just under 10,000 dwt but very comfortable and fast for her type and size in those days. Our orders were to proceed Bremen and load a full cargo of anthracite for Vitoria in Brazil a sixteen-day passage all rather good. On arrival at Bremen I felt very apprehensive about the coming voyage. Although the trip from Amsterdam to Bremen let me get to know the ship. The second officer pointed out to me that part of the stability information gave cause for concern. The officers who brought the ship from Japan had reason to doubt the after draft marks (These are the figures on the bow and stern post which tell you how deep the ship is in the water and are essential to obtaining correct stability calculations). That wasn't all he told me unfortunately. Apparently the captain was overheard complaining to the chief engineer when he was given my CV over the telephone by the personnel department. The captain was alleged to have told personnel "He didn't want any passenger ship chief officer prancing about in white gloves like someone out of Burtons window. He wanted a chief officer who could run the ship and the cargo."

Having got an idea of what the captain was thinking of me I must confess I was rather annoyed to say the least. During loading operation that evening I was very upset. I began to think it was wrong to come back to sea. I should have stayed at home and tried to rebuild my shipping company. I was extremely tired I just hadn't come to grips with working such long hours and suffering lack of sleep to the extent one does at sea. One soon comes to accept it as far as one can. The loading was continuing quite well when I said to the officer in charge of the deck. "I'll just take a walk aft and read the draft." I went down the gangway onto the quay and walked aft toward the stern. I never looked at the draft marks I walked past them and just wondered away past the dock entrance to the main road. At the main road I wondered far along it walking aimlessly along it past and old German air-raid shelter. I couldn't help thinking how the poor people must have suffered in it during the blitz on Germany. Knowing what Belfast suffered which was little compared to Germany. I came to a park gate, which was open. I just wandered into the park and sat down.

In my pocket I had a few marks but why I don't know I also had my Diner Card. All kinds of wild ideas passed through my mind. I thought of just going to the airport and flying home to hell with everything I'll do that. I never worried about passports I had got away with that problem before I could it again. I was beginning to get somewhat depressed and totally fed up with everything now. The past was beginning to catch up with me. I had a few Valium in my pocket, I availed myself of one just as a duck came out of the water flying along the path from the pond about ten centre meters above the ground. Another one came after it chasing it when it caught up with the other duck it caught it with its beak about the neck and pulled it to the ground. It then climbed unto the helpless duck and commenced to have its nookey. As it was enjoying its nookey another duck came flying along knocking it of the back the first duck. It then climbed on for a bit of nookey too. I couldn't stop laughing, I'm sure the German people walking about thought I was of my head. The whole episode brought me to my senses. I was out of the park and away back to my ship at a rate of knots. When I got onboard I felt rather shaken and surprised with myself at what I had done.

The captain asked to be called thirty minutes before the completion of loading and to arrange sailing for one hour after completing loading. I called him thirty minutes before finishing cargo as he requested and was rather surprised to see he wasn't turned in but was lying on his settee. On completion I went up to tell him how much cargo we had loaded. He looked at me his face getting red and even more red as he looked at me, suddenly he yelled. "You've made a bloody a balls of the cargo." He dashed out onto the deck; I could hear him shouting to the crew not to close the hatch but to get them open again.

"Get the bloody fore man get the cargo going again".

He really was going mad. In the mean time I had the second officer check my final figure. "Yes", he said.

"Nothing wrong with those calculations that is what I thought the final would be."

"That is why the old man is going mad out there he reckons my figures are all wrong. I think he is up in his cabin now, I'll better go and see him, but I'm about to explode and I don't care who he is but I'll just go home and refuse to sail. I don't care what happens now." Anyway I went up to his cabin and demanded he check my figures and let me see his. He snatched mine out of my hand, studied them and then fell into his chair and said.

"Oh Christ what have I done, what have I done. I've made an awful balls of all this. I forgot we had full bunkers for a round trip to South America".

He dashed out of his cabin again on to the deck to get the cargo stopped. I waited in his cabin until he came back and when he did. He looked so terrible, so humiliated looking. He looked at me like a very naughty pup. Taking my hand he said.

"Ralph I'm so sorry truly I am, I'm sorry I mistrusted you and shouted at you." I said "Captain for

God sake forget it, you've overloaded the ship what are you intending to do about that? "The Germans will crucify you if you attempt to sail overloaded on the other hand it will cost thousands of pounds to get cranes to start discharging what you overloaded plus of course the delay to the ship."

"I'll go and get the draft again and calculate how much you have overloaded us by."

This I did as quickly as I could. The second officer took the density of the dock water again. I reckoned he only overloaded us by less that an inch. By the time the cargo had been loaded again the stevedores hardly had any time to get cargo into us.

"You've overloaded us by less than an inch."

He looked at me rather sheepishly and said.

"Would you sail rather than make a whole song and dance about this."

I thought the old man was retiring at the end of his next trip. If he ends up in court after overloading the ship. He will be finished. I really felt so sorry about it all for his sake. I said, "If the second officer agrees to sail I will also."

I wasn't going to let him blame me for overloading the ship at some time in the future. I wanted a witness to it all without making a whole 'song and dance about the episode'.

The pilot came aboard and said. "Captain you haven't ordered tugs yet," said the pilot.

"I don't want tugs we can do without them."

We cleared the locks and headed out into the River Weser for the North Sea. I was exhausted by this time when the wee captain came onto the bridge and said.

"Ralph, you didn't get any sleep this last couple of days. You go and get your head down, I'll do your watch."

We had sailed from Amsterdam short handed because the third officer didn't join until Bremen. I went below and got my head down for a sleep.

I had a great sleep and when I eventually took up my next watch I was surprised that we were as far down the North Sea as we were. The Texel Light was on our port side and for some reason or other I felt really good. There we were deep laden and bound down to South America, Brazil actually, with the sea like glass and hardly a breath of wind. You know I really felt I had escaped from something what I don't know. Now I knew what the wee budgie must feel like when he gets out of his cage. The Radio Officer (Sparkey) handed me a cable, which I didn't like at all, until I read it. My wife had just been awarded her degree in History and Russian Studies from Queens University, Belfast after many years hard work as a mature student. Immediately I sent her a large bouquet, I was really delighted for her. At the back of her mind all the time as she studied was concern for what was going to become of me.

It seemed like yesterday since I had come back to sea. We were outward bound for South America. So much had happened to me over the past few years that now it all seemed to be a dream. As we came down the southwest-shipping lane I felt I had never been away from the sea.

In about another four days whites will be the order of the day. We shall be passing the Azores when the weather should be really good at this time of the year. On Sunday morning after captain's inspection of accommodation and stores it was the custom for the captain to invite the chief engineer and the chief officer to his cabin for drinks before lunch. I think prelunch drinks may have been the forerunner of the 'management meeting idea' some shore superintendent thought of it in the Merchant Navy and adopted it for shore industry. What I do know is that during that half hour in the old mans cabin there is more planning and discussion about the voyage done than at any other time.

I had just completed plotting my star sights when I felt rather ill. The old man came on the bridge just before breakfast; he came straight over to me and asked. "Are you ok, mate"?

"Do I look that bad"?

"You look as though you've seen a ghost," He replied. As soon as I was relieved by the forenoon watch, the third officer. I skipped breakfast and went strait to bed. I was called for my watch again in the afternoon at 1530 and again at one bell 1545. When I arrived on the bridge at 1555 I couldn't stand up I was so faint. The second officer called the captain who insisted that I get turned in again, which I did. Some captains are very competent when it comes to medical problems others just hate medical problems and don't want to know. Unfortunately ours was of the latter ilk. Give him credit he took my watch some captains would have put the officers on watch and watch, that is relieving each other. I was under the weather for four days. Whilst I did take over my duties as soon as the dizzy fits cleared up I never really felt the best, health wise. A ship is no place to be sick; everyone has too much work to do without carrying out other crewmembers duties.

On arrival at Vitoria the captain had arranged for me to attend a clinic in a local hospital. The old man insisted in accompanying me to the hospital. I was questioned at great length by the doctor and given a thorough examination and told I must come back again in the morning for a second examination after the results of the blood tests. It was a doctor who spoke English with a strong American accent who examined me. The hospital was a large public hospital. It seemed rather oppressive if not foreboding in some ways. After being confined to a ship for the past twenty days. The hospital had an air about it of being full of obese women and unwashed children. The noise of people shouting to each other and kids crying was somewhat trying to say the least. One good point was our wee captain didn't offer to accompany me to the hospital again the next morning. On my next visit to the clinic I was questioned at great length about drugs. I assured the doctor I did not take any drugs but that I had been taking perhaps rather more valium than I should have up until about six to eight weeks ago. He was of the opinion that I had come off Valium much too quickly and should have eased myself of the drug. I got the impression that he thought I was being somewhat economical with the truth. His opinion was that I was off Velum long enough to be clear of any after effects now so he was abit mystified. However the tablets he gave be to clear my blood he assured me would solve all my medical problems and they did too.

When I arrived onboard I took the doctors letter up to the captain. He seemed very pleased when he read it. He beckoned me to sit down. "I have instructions for you from the company which should make you happy. On arrival back in the UK you are to pay off and join the *Ashington* as master in South Shields. By the time the *Washington* arrives home the *Ashington* should be in drydock. Please ensure that Potts is fully conversant with the company's accountancy system and operation policy when he leaves your ship. A superintendent will visit him when he settles into his command before leaving the Tyne. All his questions can be answered including salary etc then. Please wish him all the very best on his promotion assuring him of our support at all times.

"Well Ralph that was the quickest promotion I ever came across. I must say I'm pleased, that for once in that office they took some cognisance of the report I radioed to them".

"Captain I too am pleased they paid attention to your cable and may I thank you for your trust and confidence in me to send such a cable in the first place."

He shook hands with me suggesting that I come back at one bell and bring the chief with me and we'll drink to your new command. That is exactly what I did. As I knocked on the captains door and stepped in to his cabin. He said. "Have a seat gentlemen I have news for you both."

CHAPTER FOURTEEN

"Upon completion of discharge we are to load a full cargo of 'Pig Iron' at this berth for a two port discharge. Immingham and Gdansk, Poland." He lifted his eyes of the orders as he read them and said. "That is really lovely, we don't have to shift ship to load. Chief you know our chief officer has been promoted to captain upon arrival in the UK. Lets drink to that, when we can find the bloody bottle.

"You know Ralph, Tommy here was chief engineer of the *Ashington* for quite some time. Isn't that correct Tommy?" The chief looked at me and nodded.

"Ralph, she has seen her day but she is a really lovely old ship and a man like you will get the best out of her and enjoy her."

"Before we go down to lunch, Captain, what about you and I and the chief going ashore to-night and treating ourselves to one of these Brazilian steaks."

"Ralph I think that would be a good idea. Did you hear that Tommy? A run ashore to night the three of us"

"Yes certainly captain, my cabin at 1930 for a 'tipple' first."

After tea I had a good shower and broke out a new shirt. I really felt fresh and ready for a little socialising as I sat down in the chief's cabin with a nice cool Gin and Tonic.

"Being on the south side of the river we will have to get a local to row us across the river in one of the wee boats."

"You're a gypsy, chief." Said the old man with a bit of a smile. A channel runs through the town dividing the city from the abject poverty of the shantytown on the south side. Vitoria is on an island in the Espirito Santo Bay, which is linked to the mainland by a bridge. It was the south side where we discharged our cargo and would load our homeward cargo of 'pig iron'

There was a few of the locals with little rowing boats squabbling among themselves for the privilege of rowing the three of us across the river and earning a few 'Reals' preferably US dollars and of course the ubiquitous packet of English cigarettes. I confess I was none too happy when the three of us stepped into the wee boat. When the crewman got in with his oars the freeboard (the distance of the edge of the boat from the water) was about 6 centre meters.

We were away across the river before we realized it. No doubt our oarsman knew the crew would becoming ashore soon and had to get back quickly for more business. We decided to walk into town, as it wasn't too far.

The buildings all seemed to be old colonial; the whole place seemed to have an interesting air about it. We soon found a rather nice hotel with a lovely restaurant. In we went and found the maitre D' and a nice table were we could watch all the style coming and going. All though our stake's were big and quite good they were nothing compared to a good porterhouse stake back home in Northern Ireland. The more I tried to explain this to my colleagues the more they were convinced I had kissed the Blarney stone. Anyway the old man suggested we eat up and find a bar with a bit of life in it. Of we went along the road a few blocks to what seemed to be just the place for a couple of mariners who had spent the last few weeks onboard a ship smelling of fuel oil and constant cooking. A quick inspection revealed we were the only males in the place with quite a few young ladies sitting about. Tommy elbowed me gently saying. "Don't stare Ralph you'll have a heart attack." A couple of these girls had dresses which only had a back and front to them, the sides being just very wide lacing. They really did look stunning having the body that could carry such a dress. All the other girls were also very provocatively dressed. The penny very soon dropped, we had landed ourselves in what was liable to turn out to be a clip joint. A quick conference decided we should vacate the premises soonest.

We all had had nasty experiences in various parts of South America during our sea careers through visiting such places. The police seem to arrive from nowhere accusing the poor seafarer of all sorts of criminal activity. The innocent seamen having to find his way back to his ship with a very sore head and penniless. A couple of the ladies came over to our table asking would we like company. The chief pointed to the captain and said, "Our dad here is to old for your type of company". The old man nearly had an apoplectic fit. Anyway we left and found another bar come restaurant, which was a girly bar also, but I think they looked at us and decided we were old and decrepit at least they didn't bother us. The rum and coke was good so we stayed. The old man said laughingly. "If this is what is on offer here in Vitoria we had better get the needles in the medical locker sharpened, for the run home." "Oh! For the days of the M&B's much easier than spearing backsides," said I. The chief suggested that perhaps we have had enough to eat and drink to night. We still had to find a local to row us across the water to our ship. "OK lets go," said the captain, as he stood up a little unsteady on his feet. Out we strode along the road to the little landing stage were an oarsman lay sleeping in his rowing boat. "Senor" shouted the chief in his best Spanish notwithstanding the fact we were in a Portuguese speaking country. The boatman nearly jumped out of his skin, as he beckoned us to take a seat in his wee boat. He soon had us across the water to where the *Washington* was berthed. The deck watch on the gangway welcomed us onboard, enquiring as to our jollifications ashore. The old man invited us up to his cabin for a nightcap, which of course we couldn't refuse. Just as the rum was about to come out my ears I stood up and wished everyone goodnight suggesting that we must do that again sometime.

The morning seemed to come early as my steward called me with a cup of hot tea and a little toast. I jumped out of my bunk to get into the shower quickly knowing the bos'un would soon be at the office for his day's orders. It was my intention also to instruct the officers as to how I wanted the holds prepared to receive our cargo of 'pig iron'. There being little or no dust from billets of pig iron it would be a good idea to get the crew over the side on stages and get the hull (ships side) painted. For that operation a discussion with the bos'un was necessary. After breakfast everyone seemed to be very busy. The second officer was engaged in his chart corrections whilst the third officer was preparing to overhaul the life-saving equipment, which included the lifeboats, a big job in itself. I reminded them by tomorrow morning we should complete discharge and commence getting the ship ready to start loading for home. At this time of the day only the radio officer could indulge himself in sight seeing ashore.

The following day we commenced to prepare the holds for loading. The captain under no circumstances, would he allow us to wash the holds, a good sweep was all he would permit. The excess wash water in the holds would have to be pumped over the side. The previous cargo being anthracite the excess water would look like oil and the ship would be very heavily fined for pollution. In which case the old man and myself risked a jail sentence. The holds seemed very clean as the crew did an excellent job of the sweeping. Next morning a rather rickety train commenced to shunt rail wagons alongside upon which was our cargo. Loading soon commenced, for a few packets of cigarettes the stevedores would be most obliging. Pig Iron being very heavy it was most important to ensure that the cargo was not dropped from a height into the ship but practically set unto the tank tops (the bottom of the holds). Hence ensuring there would be no damage to either the ship or the cargo. I considered it not very clever to relay on dunnage alone to protect the ship and cargo.

In a few days we were down to our marks, loaded and ready for home. If one lived in Ireland as I did loading for an English port was not going home unless one was leaving the ship and travelling to Ireland on leave. Soon we had a pilot onboard and the tugs alongside. With very little effort we were of the berth and outward bound. Passed the iron ore port of Tubarao where giant bulkcarriers lay loading iron ore for Europe and Japan. Tubarao was miles from anywhere. I felt rather sorry for the crews on those ships they were at the ends of the earth. At least we are small enough to get into most ports. Soon we disembarked the pilot and cleared Espirito Santo Bay with only 5,080 miles to steam to the Humber. We should pick up the Humber pilot in about seventeen days.

The weather was beautiful once again; it would be too much to expect that the weather would be like this throughout the homeward bound passage as it was outward bound. Just to get the grey matter out of my head I prepared four evening stars for sights using my 'Rude Star' identifier. Just as I took the ships sextant out of its box the old man appeared on the bridge. I knew something was on his mind.

"Ralph, as you know it has been sometime since I was foreign-going, because of my pilot licences it has been more economical for the company to keep me on the short sea trades. Would you like to take over the hospital? The chief steward will still do the minor work but I would like you to do the more serious work."

"Yes certainly I'll be pleased to do that, but you would still do the burials if any of the important pages are missing from the 'Ships Captains Medical Guide' though." He just grinned and left the bridge.

Next morning at 0800 as I came off the bridge I put my head into the Chief Stewards cabin and told him the old man had said he wanted me to do the more serious medical cases. The Chief Steward just looked at me and said. "Yes he has told me so, he hasn't been foreign because of his licences for sometime now. The poor old bugger hates the idea of having to start giving injections after being in Brazil" "I can understand that but he has forgotten I haven't been at sea for quite sometime, not that that would worry him. Anyway, call me if you want me but if we have a run of medical problems we'll have a surgery at 1000 each morning at the hospital, ok."

After breakfast I had my usual walk around the ship to see how the Bos'un was getting on with getting the ship painted up for arrival back in the UK. The sea was like glass which we were making the best of by having the crew aloft painting the masts and white leading the rigging. I had arranged with the captain to have my first lesson in the companies accounting system at 1000. I was just about to make a real start to it when the steward arrived with our coffee. By the time we finished coffee and opened the blue book (the official book in which the crew wages were recorded) the chief engineer arrived. It was soon time for morning prayers (a wee tot of rum). I could see it was going to take sometime to come to grips with this accountancy system.

Sunday morning and time for captain's inspection of accommodation and ships stores. The captain, myself, chief engineer and chief steward followed the old man round the ship inspecting everywhere and everything, duly making notes in our note books of any short comings. Afterwards we all retired to the captain's cabin for morning prayers and to sign the ships official log book in the appropriate columns to the affect that all was well in accordance with the Merchant Shipping Acts. I must say to-date I had enjoyed very much my first trip back to sea after my years ashore in business. My shipmates were all totally unpretentious and very genuine. I think the esprit de corps among a crew is something people ashore would just never understand. Especially in comparison with the cut throat life of business.

CHAPTER FIFTEEN

We were soon running up the channel in typical English summer weather at sea, dense fog both radars going together with the whistle blowing and the top knocked off the speed. The watch doubled and everyone feeling a little on edge. I was concerned as we were sailing in the inshore traffic zone, which at that time was somewhat in contention. Keeping to traffic lanes was something which came into vogue when I was ashore in business. Because of the attitude of the courts to cases occurring in the inshore zones. Using the inshore traffic zone or keeping out in the traffic lanes was not too clear as to what was the correct course of action. Eventually our Officers Association advised that we should treat the inshore traffic zone as a no go area. I didn't want the old man to think I was totally ignorant of the rules of using these comparatively new traffic rules. I was nevertheless keen to know what he felt about it all. So I raised the question rather gently with him. Captain said I. "What is your opinion of using the inshore zones vis~vis the traffic lanes out side"?

"Funny you should ask that question mate. I'm just thinking to myself. Is it correct to use the inshore zone all the way along the coast? Or should I be over on the French Coast using the northeast bound traffic lane and then crossing over at the 'Fairy West' buoy to the north bound lane up to the Humber? Ralph I'm really not sure If what we are doing now is wrong I will need to re-mortgage the house to pay the fine."

"Anyway not to worry captain the fog is starting to clear. I can see that ship fine on the starboard bow about four cables ahead now. There is another one ahead of him; yes it is clearing for sure".

"I think mate we will go over to the North East bound lane to pass through the Straits, Just take her over there now."

"I'll just put a fix on the chart now, sir and take her over". The third officer would soon relieve me for my tea as it was coming up to 1700. I could hear the steward ring the tea bell and immediately the third officer stepped unto the bridge.

"What's on offer down there three/oh? A nice steak maybe?"

"No it's not Sunday yet Ralph."

Sunday night was always steak night at sea in a good ship and in a really good ship a glass of wine to help it down.

When I did come off watch I spent my time packing. I had been ordered to get to the Tyne as soon as I could to take command of the *Ashington*. By tomorrow morning we should be tied up at Immingham and I should be paid off and on my way to the station to catch a train to Newcastle. It so happened we did tie up on time as planned. I had hardly signed off the ship when a taxi arrived alongside which had been ordered by the agent to get me to the train station as quickly as possible. Upon arrival at Newcastle I took a taxi down to South Shields I was so tired I thought, 'to hell with expense.' I had hawked my gear about enough to day. I didn't know where one would get a train to South Shields.

As I got out of the taxi a very kind and obliging lad came over to me and shook hands.

"Let me help you with that gear captain."

He lifted one of my cases and headed for the gangway. I took the other one and followed him. "By the way sir, I'm the second officer on duty to-night. The crew are joining tomorrow I understand. There is a small catering staff onboard the rest will join in the morning. The cook left a hot meal for you in the hot press before he went home. If you just follow me I'll show you to your cabin."

She may be an old ship but she was beautiful. The wood panelling in my cabin was so well polished that I could see my reflection in it on the bulkhead. I found my way to the officer's saloon and pantry. There in the pantry was a huge steak and kidney pie with the usual trimmings and Garfield potatoes. Very nice I thought and I was really ready for it. The duty engineer appeared in the doorway he was about to get himself a cup of tea.

"Are you the new captain he enquired"?

"I am"

I replied putting forth my hand to shake his extended hand.

"You'll love this old ship, no chrome and plastic here captain all brass and tropical hardwood."

He ventured as he handed me a large cup of tea. I noticed the bulkheads in the public rooms were all highly polished and of tropical hardwood. Each panel of hardwood had a little label in wood depicting the type of wood the panel was made from. The brass portholes were also highly polished "Yes the interior is really beautiful but I think the carpets have seen better days". I was really impressed but I will have a good look at her tomorrow I thought. The next day I had a really good inspection of the whole ship. She had been well cared for from 1957 her year of build. I went up to the bridge into the chartroom and wheelhouse I couldn't help feeling it was like something out of a John Wayne film set. All the wheelhouse windows opened using a leather strap like an old railway carriage, but she was a solid old ship with lots of character.

Just as I went below to my cabin I met the chief engineer a really charming man. As I shook hands with the chief I knew I would enjoy this mans company. He was a little hard of hearing sometimes necessitating repeating ones self from time to time. He assured me it would be a week before we would have the engines ready to go to sea. I thought to my self, good I'll get my wife over for a few days. Before commencing to sign the crew on I went to the phone and asked her to come over to the ship. She was delighted to do so provided she could bring our youngest son with her, as there was no one at home to look after him. We had friends who could accommodate our daughter. The following day I met Sheelagh and Michael at Newcastle airport. The new Seaman Mission had a block of accommodation for officers, which was very pleasant and very comfortable so we decided to stay there instead of onboard a ship in drydock. When a ship is in a drydock calls of nature usually require a trip ashore to a loo some distance from the ship. Hence accommodation ashore is much more suitable especially at night.

Some of the crew joined, not all; the remainder would join a couple of days before sailing. On the nice summer evenings we were able to take a bus into Sunderland then change buses for somewhere of interest. We spent a lovely day in Durham visiting the cathedral and the university. A visit to the Abbey at Tynemouth was also of interest. Most of the Abbeys in northern England had been built my monks originating from Ulster. Whilst I was working the family was able to go shopping in Newcastle especially Eldon Court. Actually we made the most of our few days together. One Saturday afternoon whilst finishing of some paperwork I left my young son to explore the ship by himself. He came dashing into my cabin all excited; his eyes were standing on his head. "Dad, dad" he said, "I saw a girl with no clothes on" he then proceed to describe the young lady in great detail. It just dawned on me then who she was. One of the crew had been given permission for his lady friend to visit the ship. She had just stepped from the showers to run along the alleyway to her boyfriend's cabin not knowing Michael had been left to prowl about. It was my entire fault, as I should have instructed the young lad to keep out of the crew accommodation. It took him a very long time to get over it not that he ever wanted to.

Sailing day approached when I left the family back to the airport and said all our goodbyes in the usual time honoured way. When I arrived back onboard I couldn't wait to get to sea. I had had enough of waiting to get away from the repair yard. I had offered to swing the compasses when we sailed off Tynemouth but the company declined my offer. I supposed being so new to the company they the company didn't quite trust the new boy. Our orders were suddenly changed the plan was to proceed up the river to a loading berth and there load a full cargo of coal for a Hamburg Power Station, swinging compasses after loading of Tynemouth. The cargo was loaded in a couple of days and we were soon underway for Hamburg. I was glad of the sea air the only problem I had was the chief engineer had to keep his radio rather loud because of his hearing problem. It wasn't too bad really because he was really only interested in the cricket scores.

On arrival at Hamburg I had decided to go into Saint Pauli, as I hadn't been in Hamburg for many years. The change to the whole city was amazing. I first visited Hamburg in early 1950. The sight, which remained in my mind for many years, was that of the number of men who were limbless with their torso on what we as children called a ball bearing guider. That was a wooden board with a ball bearing wheel at each corner. On some boards the for'ard two wheels were on a piece of wood or stick bolted to the board with a single bolt which could be manoeuvred with a piece of rope to facilitate turning. The limbless person then propelled themselves along by their hands wearing heavy gloves. It didn't take a genius to figure out that these poor souls were war-wounded men left very much to fend for them in a war torn country. That was five years after the ending of hostilities. Even in 1950 cigarettes were still a very important source of currency should visitors to the country wish to purchase German military memorabilia. It was a beautiful evening for a walk but I only walked as far as the Bismarck statute, which was really a fair distance. I just sat down in the small park at the statute and watched the style go past. Watching people in all their style walk past is one of my most enjoyable pastimes. I always enjoyed going for a good walk after tea when in port. Unfortunately I always forget when one goes for a walk and you reach your turning point, you have to walk all the way back again to reach to your starting point. When I got back onboard I was ready for my bunk and a good sleep. It is a long way down the river Elbe again and as master I am expected to be on the bridge at all times in restricted navigation. The agent had advised us that we should be away again by the following evening if not sooner.

Our next port of call would be Mo-I-Rana in Northern Norway just below the Arctic Circle to load a full cargo of pig iron for Antwerp. My orders were as usual to get there as soon as possible. The spread of lay days was very small (that is the period in which I must give notice to the shippers that the ship is in all respects ready to commence loading the cargo, otherwise the contract of afreightment becomes void able.). I was very concerned about time because the swell on the Norwegian Coast can be considerable and this old ship could only make 11 knots. Pushing against the swell going up the coast was going to be difficult. There was no suggesting at this time to use the leads (The inshore passage up the Norwegian Coast). To use the leads can be expensive because of the cost of pilotage.

By the afternoon again we had the pilot onboard and tugs alongside. Soon we were underway down the Elbe bound for Mo-I-Rana in Norway. It is a boring passage down the Elbe like most continental rivers except on Sunday afternoons when the river seems to be festooned with yachts manned by uninhibited blond frauleins. We had the ebb tide with us for most of the way down the river so it didn't seem to long until the pilot cutter was alongside and we were waving the pilot away. Once pass the Elbe light float we headed north for the Norwegian coast about three and half days passage to Mo-I-Rana weather permitting. The next day we were pushing a long low swell and speed was down to ten knots with the lay days lessening all the time. It can be rather difficult at times to find the entrance to some of the Fjords on the Norwegian coast. At night there are so many alternating and occulting lights, which can be difficult to distinguish hence the Norwegian coast is not really the navigators favourite coast.

Soon we were passing the mooring lines ashore and making fast in Mo-I-Rana with just hours to spare to tender 'notice of readiness'. Except for the steel mills the rest of the countryside looked idyllic. Loading commenced almost at once. On the third day loading was complete. Considerable time was spent tombing and securing the cargo as we expected to roll heavily and violently. Because of the design of the ship, just a single deck all the weight was in the bottom of the ship which stability wise made her a very stiff ship in a seaway. We were soon on our way down the Fjord to the North Atlantic. Having disembarked the pilot we steered west clear of the coast. Once clear course was altered to the south'ard and the Port of Antwerp.

The weather turned bad a very heavy southwesterly sea was running with a big swell. The strains and groans of the old ship was becoming deafening. It was very difficult to find a comfortable course for her and still make good headway to the south. The rolling was violent at times necessitating 'heaving too' as best one could, especially to take the strain of the engine. I think this manoeuvre brought a smile to the chief's face.

Eventually we passed down the North Sea to the Schouwenbank, the tide being high I was able to enter the Schelde from the northwest. We changed pilots at Flushing for the run up the river to Antwerp. There is not a seaman in Christendom who likes the trip up the Schelde to Antwerp. It is a long windy passage needing constant attention. Should the weather come in foggy the river passage becomes hazardous. By the time one leaves the bridge one is really suffering considerable fatigue. At arrival of the locks it is nothing to be kept waiting for hours for your turn to enter the locks. Having entered the locks it can be up to an hour before your ship can be cleared into the vast Antwerp dock system and another hour to pass through the system to your berth. From the 'A1'bouy at the Schelde Pilot station to tie-up up at your berth in Antwerp can be anything up to twenty hours during which the whole of that time is spent on your feet on the bridge. Not withstanding the fact the captain could have spent many days on the bridge either on passage up the channel or coming down the North Sea to the 'A1'bouy at the entrance to the river Schelde.

The cargo was destined for further inland in Germany. This meant waiting for barges to receive our cargo for the river passage into Germany. I had considerable ships business to attend to in town. Therefore I arranged with the ships agent to send a car for me next morning to take me into town. It is the business of a captain to 'note protest' upon arrival in port. That is he must present himself in front of a 'Notary Public' with his log book to swear that any damage to his cargo was caused by an 'Act of God' and not his lack of care and attention or bad seamanship or an unseaworthy ship. In Antwerp however it is not just a case of presenting oneself in front of a 'Notary the Belgium's like to have a little court case about the matter just to be different.

I always liked Antwerp ever since I was boy. There is plenty to see what ever your interests might be and even more to do especially after sunset. The antique and art shops, nautical bric-a-brac and paintings of old sailing ships were always worth finding. A wander along 'Skipper Straat' which was always most intriguing especially for a young lad. Alas! The sun had long crossed the yardarm. The bar with the dance band, comprised, of robots was gone since I was a boy or maybe I was passed being capable of finding it. I thought one thing I must do is have a good sleep before sailing. It is a long stand-by all the way from the berth in the Antwerp docks until ones ship clears the South Goodwin Light. It can be eighteen hours, more if the tide is against you most of the way down the Schelde. If visibility is bad, which it often is it can be extremely strenuous having ones head buried in a radar, set for so long in heavy traffic. We sailed from our berth in Antwerp late at night and spent almost an hour waiting our turn for the lock to be turned back to let us into the river. Eventually our turn came when we cleared the locks and entered the river. Morning was slowly breaking in the eastern sky as the steward arrived on the bridge with plates of lovely brown toast for the pilot and I and the officer of the watch.

"I always take tea on an English ship" said the pilot, "I really enjoy English tea, captain." "You will get tea with your toast in a minute pilot" I said.

We were bound in ballast down the river to Le Havre to load grain for Tilbury. The ships holds had to be spotless to load such a cargo and to pass the French government grain inspector. The crew would soon be called to commence washing the holds and clean the bilges and test them to the satisfaction of the chief officer. The chief officer would still be expected to stand a watch. When loading grain intricate grain calculations are required to ensure the ship has sufficient stability at all time during the voyage to be safe. I always made it a practise to also do stability calculations when loading grain as a cross check for the chief officer. These calculations have to be on the proper forms and presented to the local port authorities before sailing.

The weather as we dropped the pilot was very promising which augured well for a nice passage to Le Havre. Our pilot came onboard by helicopter, which was an experience for me but was very efficient. It wasn't long before we were approaching our berth behind a German ship, which was also about to load a cargo of grain for somewhere. The agent and the shore officials were soon onboard. The loading arrangements were that we should commence loading after the German ship, which was berthed ahead of us, which would be tomorrow morning after breakfast. That all sounded lovely a nice quiet peaceful night onboard before starting loading tomorrow. The chief and I decided on a nice walk ashore and a beer at a sidewalk café. It was September and there was still warmth in the evening air. That is just what we did a pleasant stroll ashore and a few beers. I was hoping to get to the UK as soon as possible because my leave was due and I was looking forward to it very much.

When we did arrive back onboard after our walk the ship was loading. The chief officer came up to my cabin to inform me there had been a change of loading plan whilst I was ashore. The ship ahead of us on the berth had some sort of difficulty with its stability calculations. Hence the French authorities refused to let her load until she presented her grain loading plan and supporting calculations. In the meantime they took us ahead of her for loading as our chief officer had everything ready to start loading the cargo. That all meant we would get away sooner. We should be ready to sail tomorrow evening all being well. I got on the phone to the chief engineer. He was delighted as it was only about eighteen hours from here to Tilbury.

After breakfast the agent came onboard to advise me that the stevedores anticipated completing loading about 1800 this evening. When would I be willing to sail. I told him one hour after completion of loading. "Mr agent, you can order one tug and the pilot for one hour after completion of cargo. All going well I should be at Tilbury grain silos in about eighteen hours after disembarking our outward pilot. I want to get some perfume for my wife. Where do you suggest"? The agent sat down again and opened his brief case took out a pad of some sort and made a note on it. As he handed it to me he gave me instructions as to how to find the shop, as it was I knew where the shop was. Captain, he said this note will save you some money, I will see you later this evening. As we shook hands he smiled and said to me "Perhaps captain you would like some wine, what would you like"? "That is very kind of you sir, as long as it flows I will enjoy it". With a wave of the hand he was away ashore. I lifted my phone and called the chief to advise him I had a note from the agent to get a discount on perfume at one of the shops. He immediately suggested he come with me and avail himself of the offer also. The two of us went off up the road to find the shop. As I reached the gangway I noticed the chief officer looking down number three hold. I called him and asked if he would like me to get him some perfume for his wife? "Yes that would be very nice indeed 'Arpege' if you can but don't spend more that £50. Would you like the money now"? "No time enough when I get back"

We found the shop and went in. Two lovely girls stepped forward to serve us. I in my very best Ulster French said "Je voudrais du parfum, s'il vous plait." and handed her the note the agent gave me. The chief then burst out laughing for some reason. Je ne parle pas bien francais. I then spoke in English and she immediately suggested we converse in English she spoke beautiful English. The two girls couldn't do enough for us. We got about 30% discount, which was very good, and I only spent about £40 for the chief officer. I found out why the chief thought me funny in the shop, he spoke almost fluent French having worked in North Africa for a time.

The agent as promised arrived onboard just as the crew were battening down the hatches preparing for sea. He brought me two cases of wine, which was very well accepted. An hour sooner and we would have demolished the lot at teatime. All the necessary paperwork dealt with and duly signed we shook hands and off he went ashore. I heard the second officer take the pilot unto the bridge and the mate call to the crew on deck "Stations, Fore and Aft" I wondered up to the bridge a bit excited as this was now the last homeward leg of the voyage. Not just home to England for the ship but I was going right home to Ireland.

Twenty hours later and my relieve came up the gangway at Tilbury. I was delighted to see him and watch him sign the logbook for the ship.

CHAPTER SIXTEEN

I HAD ARRIVED HOME after my first trip back to sea since being in business. It was a great relief to be home but I knew I was coming home to deal with a lot of financial problems from my days as a business gnome. My wife had had a lot of decoration done around the house for me coming home a task for which I was forever in her debt because I hated decorating. The thought of spending a leave decorating was far beyond the pale even though parts of the walls in the lounge had been left like a relief map of Tibet. One of the major problems of going to sea and having a family was the work and responsibilities left for ones wife to deal with. I went out one evening with my wife for a drink and a yarn at our local. She related a story to me about the time when I was trading in the Pacific. I think the time in question would have been about when I was in China, however, our young daughter, just a baby was very ill about 2:00 am when the doctor was needed. My wife couldn't get the duty doctor who was a locum to come out to the house. Eventually she got dressed and went to his home in the early hours of a cold wet morning to try and plead with him to come up to the house and see the child.

He refused and sent her away with a flea in her ear. It was as much as she could do to see her own way home through her tears, which were tripping her. She did what she could for the child when later in the morning after breakfast the doctor called full of remorse. As she related the story to me, I felt so sorry for her I was nearly in tears. But that is the life of a seafarer's wife. She runs the home in everyway and the longer her husband stays at sea the more she becomes very professional at everything to do with the home including repairs. When the husband comes home on leave she will only pay lip service to his views and ideas, he is very much the passenger in the house like it or not. There is an element of escapism in the life of a seafarer.

Seafaring is a very stressful life particular so in wintertime. Usually the first few days at home one is really winding down from the tension of the voyage, what my wife always called the eggshell days. It is for that reason stories, which may give cause for concern or even mail, which may do, so was kept until the passing of the eggshell days. It was then all the problems concerning the winding up of my business, which had accumulated whilst I was at sea landed on my lap. The worst being the grim reaper the taxman. He figured he was owed thousands something equivalent to the American defence budget whereas I calculated I might owe him something equating to my Sunday morning church collection.

My wife after she got her degree was hell bent on going to work. I was not going to come home on leave to sit in the house on my own all day. Yet I could see her point the children were now able to fend for themselves. Her Majesty the Queen was looking after one of them. Like all couples we had to learn to compromise. My wife took a part time job in the Social Service and soon found that was more than enough hours to be working out.

A knock came to the door one morning whilst my wife was away at work; I was making a pot of broth. This lady, I suppose in her fifties and somewhat untidily dressed introduced herself as a tax inspector. I asked her for identification which she produced. Proving her bona fides I invited her in. She asked me endless questions as I stirred the soup I was making. Here said I as I handed her a big soup ladle.

"Keep stirring that soup whilst I discharge my ballast."

She was slightly taken aback. When I return from the loo I just let her carry on making my soup. I said to her.

"You look good making that soup," said she.

"Yes and it looks good too" and so we discussed the pro and cons of making soup. She looked at me and said. "Your supposed to have owned a shipping company did you not? I don't see any Picassos or any other valuable paintings or anything valuable at all for that matter except you maybe. What did you do with all the money"?

"Ploughed it all back into the business as I earned it. Anyway as you well know. A guy called the taxman took it all to help keep a lady in London. I think her address is Buck House" I replied.

"Well that may be so but really I don't see any display of wealth."

Just at that I heard my wife Sheelagh open the front door. I introduced her to the tax lady and repeated the tax inspector's remarks to her regarding our lack of wealth. Said Sheelagh to the inspector. "You people took it all and now I suppose your looking more?"

I knew something had to be done about the tax question but I did not agree the amount they alleged I owed. I had a discussion with the liquidator of my shipping company and with my bank executives and also friends in the accountancy profession. One suggested I should become a bankrupt another suggested I should make the Tax people think I was a man of straw and therefore not worth pursuing for the money. The aforementioned selections of methods suggested by tax experts to solve my problem only annoyed me intensely. I was not insolvent in any shape or form nor was I a man of straw. The Inland Revenue was hounding me for a sum of money I did not owe. The revenue was after me for money I maintained was not taxable. It was all a matter of law on money ploughed back into the company. I accepted that I owed a little more than £1,000 maybe £1300 but that was all. I was quite willing to pay that amount in full and final settlement but they wouldn't have it.

The problem I saw building up was going to end up in court. The revenue was going to sue for their money eventually or I was going to have to go to court for a judicial review. Possibly that may all cost more than the revenue were claiming. I thought long and hard about it all. I remember one accountant a professed tax expert saying to me. "You old sea dogs are a Wiley lot" That remark annoyed me very much it had connotations which often made me feel like doing something I would live to regret. It was a remark which was often made to me in business and which I never had the ability to laugh off.

Anyway, I said to my self 'I know what I will do' Instead of dealing with the monkeys I'll go direct to the organ grinder. I sat down and wrote a long clear explanatory letter to 10 Downing Street. I reminded the good lady in residence of her call to the nation for enterprise and effort. 'Well Mrs dear' wrote I, see what effort and enterprise has landed me with. There are few people could get a shipping company and a transport company of the ground with only £50 in their pocket and a hole in their shoe. My efforts to date have only earned me a crucifixion. Therefore your assistance in solving my problem would be much appreciated.

CHAPTER SEVENTEEN

ALL GOOD THINGS EVENTUALLY come to an end I had the usual telephone call from our personnel advising me of my next appointment. I had been appointed master of the *Pulborough* with instructions to join her on the Tyne next Monday. Time to start packing; my flights had been booked for Monday morning at 0900 Belfast to Newcastle. I supposed it would be another three months tour before I would hear from the tax people. Life was measured in tours of three months I suppose that wasn't too bad. Better than the days when one left home and had no idea when one would be home again, no such thing as being relieved abroad. You got home when your ship got home. Monday soon came round when my wife would run me to the airport.

My taxi drew up alongside the ship at the repair berth when a couple of the crew came down the gangway and took my gear out of the taxi and up the gangway to my cabin. I had just taken my coat off when a knock on the door and a voice calling. "Are you there captain?" It was the chief officer calling to introduce himself. I invited him in to my day room; we sat down and discussed the coming voyage.

Our orders were to load at Emden for Cagliari a full cargo of Anthracite thence Lipari to load a full cargo of Pumice for Aberdeen.

"At least we should see some nice weather in the Med." I suggested.

"The crew are all 'signed on' they were here last trip. There is just a few bits of stores to come so apart from the chief engineer we are already for sea."

Advised the chief officer. I think the chief engineer heard what the mate said because just as he knocked my cabin door he said. "Yes I too will be ready by tomorrow afternoon".

"So gentlemen we can provisionally arrange sailing for 1800 tomorrow, to be confirmed" they all nodded their heads in the affirmative. I walked over to the dock office to call our office and confirm with them our wish to sail at 1800 tomorrow evening. They were very pleased advising me that someone would call before noon tomorrow with the sailing papers from the customs. I strolled back to the ship only to meet the chief on his way over to the dock office to use the phone to the office. I confirmed with him that everything had been arranged for sailing at 1800 tomorrow. When I arrived back onboard I was passing the chief officers cabin. I could see him standing in his cabin deep in thought. I said

"A penny for them Basil." He looked at me and said.

"Ah I'll be glad to get away," I said to him.

"Get the shore leave notice board up as soon as possible and end shore leave at 1700 tomorrow afternoon." I went up to my cabin and got ready for tea just as the tea bell rang. The officer's saloon was another two decks down. Which was just off the smokeroom. As I went down the companionway (stairway) I thought this is really a very nice old ship. It had a very homely atmosphere about it, clean and bright too.

Next day there was much coming and going being sailing day. Nearly all the crew were from the Tyne with exception of the senior officers and the radio officer, sparkey. The chief engineer was new to the company. He was from one of the big liner companies, which was, like the rest of that class of shipping company coming to the end of its days. The chief officer, Basil was likewise but he had already done a trip. I suppose I too fell into that category. A bit of a new boy with one tour completed. It was soon nearing 1800 when the pilot could be expected to be coming along the dock. All the paper work had been completed and the lad from the office had gone ashore. I heard a knock at my door when I looked up from my desk there was the pilot. "OK. Captain are you all ready"? Asked the pilot. "Yes you just find your way up to the bridge and I'll follow," said I. The mate was just outside my cabin waiting for orders. "Stations, fore & aft, mate" I ordered. The second officer reported all the gear on the bridge had been tested and found ok. Yes,

I had heard the whistle being tested I told him. The tug was soon fast alongside, I had taken a tug on sailing as we had to swing in the river. We moved gently out into the main stream, swung and headed down river. As soon as we cleared the pier head the pilot launch was alongside and the pilot was away. Course was set for the Borkum light and the Ems. Like all the ports on the continent it is a long stand by from the sea up some god for saken river to the port. We should be there about midnight tomorrow night. I went into the chartroom and made up all my sailing cables.

One for the owners, the agents at our destination and the pilot station at the port of arrival. At least we had clear weather all the way up the river to the locks. As we lay in the lock for the lockmaster to get into the locks as many ships as possible a German submarine came into the lock. I was rather intrigued with her. On her conning tower she had the pennant number S???? Something or other I can't just remember but under the S???? She had a little U39 I think it was. As she came alongside my ship in the lock the officer on her conning tower gave me a very smart naval salute, which I returned. Actually the little episode reminded me of my days as a sea cadet. As soon as the water in the lock was level with the water in the dock the inner gates were opened and the ships in order moved out. The U-Boat moved out ahead of us, as it did so I gave her commander a hearty wave. No hard feelings for what might have happened between us thirty odd years ago.

We left the locks and moved through the dock system to our loading berth. I came off the bridge to my dayroom but couldn't get near it there were so many shore officials trying to get into my dayroom that I had difficulty getting past them all. Once I got rid of the customs, the waterfront police, chandlers etc. I was able to talk to my agent who advised me it could take a few days to load, as there were problems with rail wagons delivering the cargo. I told him not to call tomorrow unless absolutely necessary. I was going to bed and I intended to have a lie in. I turned in and slept to early afternoon. After tea I decided to take myself off for my usual walk.

I walked for some distance thinking about my bloody tax problems. I was beginning to have doubts about the wisdom of liquidating my shipping company. Maybe I should have fought harder to keep it alive. Deep within myself I was beginning to think the whole episode was affecting my health. I was very easily tired and really quite edgy not really the type of guy to get into an argument with. As I was passing a house with low windowsills, as my feet were a getting rather sore. I took off my shoes and sat on the windowsill airing my feet. A German police car passed bye not going too fast, I could hear it in the distance slowing down and turning. It soon drew up alongside me as I sat on my windowsill. The driver got out and addressed me in German; I told him that I did not speak German. He then spoke to me in perfect English. It was on the tip of my tongue to tell him

I didn't speak English only Irish that was the sort of mood I was in. He offered very kindly to run me back to my ship which I gladly accepted. I climbed up the gangway. As I passed the chief engineers cabin I could hear him and the mate having a right old laugh. I put my head round his door curtain and was immediately offered a drink. "A bicardi and coke would go down lovely," I said. As the chief poured the drink he offered some ice and lemon. I said that is the best offer I have had all night.

The 'craic' was really good, having solved the worlds economic problems I climbed the next companionway to my cabin and turned in. Whilst at breakfast the agent arrived onboard advising me that we should finish cargo about noon. I told him I would sail one hour after completion of cargo and suggested he should order one tug and the pilot for 1300 local time. The chief officer was also having breakfast he asked.

"What time shall I end shore leave"?

"Make it 1100, I bet most of the lads won't have wondered too far. This place is too expensive for man or beast, beside this berth is miles from anywhere."

I thought, funny how I'm always asked what time to end shore leave yet for years we have always ended it an hour before sailing. I suggested to the chief officer that he have a word with the chief steward and arrange a seven-bell dinner. It would be good if we could get a meal into us before we leave the berth if we could. It always takes so long to get through the locks and out into the river it is always best to get the meals over and done with if possible.

We left the berth and passed through the dock system to the locks quite gently. Only forty-five minutes in the lock until we passed out of it into the river and all the heavy river traffic. The pilot suggested we should be at the pilot station about 2200 this evening. That is when the fun starts; trying to get into the southbound shipping lanes is like trying to manoeuvre on a motorway. Why navigators forget or refuse to recognise the 'Rules of the Road' in shipping lanes is beyond my comprehension. We made a good passage down the river to the pilot station. I was soon waving to the pilot as he boarded his little pilot launch to take him over to the pilot cutter. We were now on our way to Cagliari about eight days steaming maybe nine in this ship. She doesn't have a lot of power in her old engine, which has been running since 1965.

The weather in the channel had been quite good for this time of the year and so we made a reasonable passage through the channel and down the Portuguese Coast past the Berlengas. To-night we should pass through the Straits of Gibraltar were the weather is expected to worsen. So long as the visibility remains reasonable that was my main worry. The next morning the weather was quite rough as we steamed into the Mediterranean. The Sierra Nevada's were covered in snow and looked beautiful in the strong sunlight by evening the wind had eased considerably and we began to pick up speed. A couple of days and we should be approaching Cagliari. When we did arrive at Cagliari and the pilot said we would be at least ten days discharging I was totally amazed. As we were approaching the berth I phoned the fo'c'el and gave the mate the news. Typical chief officer, all he could say was; "That is great we will be able to get the hull painted." One wonderful thing about trading to the Mediterranean is you just take your ship through the breakwater and usually your at the your berth. No long endless rivers to navigate making six to ten hour stand-bys, as is the case in north west European ports. Work started with one old crane in the morning at a rather slow rate whilst our crew spread themselves along the quayside with their man helps (long poles with paint brushes attached to facilitate painting heights) to paint the hull. I went to the agent's office and phoned our office advising them of our expected delayed discharge. I took the advantage of the agent's invitation to lunch, which was all very nice and civilised. In days gone by that was most common if not expected that the agent should invite the master out to lunch. Not now days everyone is too much in a hurry if not too mean to observe the little niceties of life, which help the days pass that more pleasantly.

I think whilst we were in Cagaliri we walked the legs of ourselves exploring the city. Apart from very interesting little shops there wasn't a great deal to do of interest to our age group. Overlooking the harbour was a very long colonnade where the populace seemed to promenade every evening. We found much enjoyment just sitting with our usual tittle after our walk each evening just watching the style go by. A couple of guys beautifully groomed complete with rather nice handbags and a dander to match walked up and down the road all evening. Just watching these pair amused us immensely. It was expected that discharging should be completed tomorrow morning. As it was imperative that the holds should be spotless to load Pumice after carrying Anthracite sailing would not be until three hours after completion of discharge, that would give the chief officer a chance to get the holds clean.

The pilot disembarked almost at the berth next day as we sailed just after breakfast. The weather was beautiful and quite warm. I sent all my sailing cables giving an eta at Lipari next day for 1000, which was perhaps being a little ambitious. About 1900 on the evening we sailed from Cagaliri the chief steward came to see me asking would I come and see one of the young ordinary seamen in his cabin. Apparently the young lad reported ill just after the afternoon smoko (tea break). As I entered his cabin, which was in darkness, I put his light on. He immediately asked me to put it out as it hurt his eyes. He looked bad and said he had been vomiting. I took his temperature, which was rather high. When I asked him to put his chin on his chest he found it painful to try and do so. Likewise when I asked him to draw his knees up to his chest. I told him we should be in Lipari before lunch tomorrow when I would have a doctor onboard to examine him.

"In the meantime get as much rest as possible and under no circumstances are you to leave this cabin except for the loo and nobody is allowed into it. You are now in quarantine from the rest of the crew".

I told the chief steward to get a notice to that effect on the door of the cabin. As we left him and walked along the alleyway out of the crew quarters. I said to the chief steward.

"I hate to say it but I think we have a case of meningitis onboard. Until we learn otherwise we will treat it as such. Establish a quarantine routine with him until further notice. I think I will give the lad a shot of penicillin, best to get the treatment started as soon as possible. Just come and give me a hand with this lot".

We went to the ships hospital and the medical locker and obtained all we needed. I took with us an ampoule of Adrenaline in case of any reaction to the penicillin.

We went back down to the boys cabin and consoled him a little. Telling him I really needed to put his bunk light on as I intended to give him an injection in his backside. At the same time enquiring if he ever had a reaction to penicillin. I didn't want to put his deckhead light on (The large cabin light) but I could hardly see the little rubber cap on the vial of penicillin powder to inject the ampoule of water into it. I turned the lad over onto his stomach and speared his stern-end. After I gave the skin where he got his injection a quick rub with a little iodine he rolled onto his back and mumbled thanks. I don't know who was the happiest he or I.

Lipari is just a small island off the Sicilian Coast it is in a group of islands including the famous Island of Stromboli. It has a couple of finger jetties, which protrude out, into the sea where ships like ours load Pumice stone for export to the world. It was about 1300 when we were all fast on the berth. Loading commenced immediately even before we had obtained clearance. The agent had a doctor with him; whilst I dealt with the ships business the chief steward took the doctor below to visit our patient. The doctor could not speak a word of English, but the agent acted as a very good interpreter. Through the agent the doctor told me he thought I was correct with my diagnoses but he could not confirm without hospital tests. In any case the sailor should be moved to hospital. I fully agreed. The agents then said he and the doctor would go ashore and make arrangements to move the patient to hospital and would return in an hour or so. In the meantime could I get the man ready to be landed ashore? His seaman's discharge book, account of wages and gear would be needed. Of course I would have it all ready for when he, the agent returned. About two hours later the agent and doctor returned with the look on their faces I knew at once there was a problem. They both looked sick, the agent immediately through his hands in the air and said. "Captain I am so, so sorry but the authorities ashore will not let the sick man land in Lipari. Not under any circumstances. They say he may contaminate our small population." A little voice said to me keep your calm boy this is not the time for a display of temper. I immediately accused the authorities of denying a sick seaman medical attention. The agent could only do as Italians are expert at doing and that is shrugging their shoulders and looking sick. I just made what I knew to be idle threats. Like radioing the British Ambassador at Rome demanding his assistance. The agent looked as though he was about to cry and when he translated my threats for the doctor he went berserk. Said the agent "I'll try once more captain God is good." In the meantime I called the mate and the chief engineer up to my cabin and had a discussion with them whilst the local boys went ashore once again to persuade the authorities to let me land the sick seaman.

"My intention is to stop all cargo and sail for the Sicilian Coast. Approach the nearest port, call the Harbour Master on the VHF and just say I have a very sick seaman needing medical attention and ask for help. They are bound to do something for me especially if I go over to say; Milazzo a big port like that would have to help me". My senior officers thought that would be a great idea instead of waiting for the Italians to make up their minds. I said "OK Chief get the engines ready and mate keep the cargo working to the last minute". Eventually the agent and the doctor arrived back onboard as sick looking as ever. "Captain" said the agent "we can't take the seaman but we will give you all the medicine you will need for him." I just looked at the agent and lifted the phone on my desk, dialled the mates cabin and ordered him to stop all cargo and batten down the hatches, I was going to sea. I rang the chief engineer and told him as soon as your ready chief were sailing.

The agent was just speechless. Two of our crew let the ropes go all at once and jumped back onboard. The stevedores were long since gone. I came astern on the engines. We just cleared the berth with ease. I had decided to go to Milazzo, which was about two hours steaming from Lipari. As soon as I was clear from Lipari I went on the VHF and called

"Milazzo Harbour, Milazzo Harbour Milazzo Harbour this is British ship Pulborough GPVE" The Harbour replied.

"Go ahead Pulborough".

"I have a very sick seaman onboard needing urgent medical attention".

"Captain come into the port and anchor."

"Thank you I will send the patient to the shore in our lifeboat ok".

"Very good captain we will be ready for you, there will be an ambulance on the quay waiting for you. Do you want a pilot"?

"No thanks I don't need a pilot". I got the chief officer to come up to the bridge and gave him strict instructions not to discuss the lad's problem. Just get him into the ambulance which will be waiting for you and get back to the ship as quickly as possible. I explained to him that I only intended to crown the anchor (that is just put the crown of the anchor on the bottom and not pay out any cable) to keep her head steady until you get back.

"Take two of the crew with you to help you and for God sake bring back the Neil Robertson stretcher use an ambulance stretcher to take him to hospital."

As soon as I eased the ship through the breakwater there was an ambulance on the quayside. The harbour was a beautiful place of Moorish architecture. Basil was away with the patient strapped to the sidebenches of the lifeboat before the anchor hit the bottom. Within what only seemed to be minutes. I saw, through my binoculars the doors of the ambulance close and Basil on his way back to us. The lifeboat was soon fast in its falls and as the anchor was being brought up so was the lifeboat. As soon as the second officer rang the anchor bell, denoting the anchor was aweigh I gave the engine a kick ahead with the wheel hard over we commenced our swing and away we went out through the breakwaters again. Clear of the breakwaters, then full ahead on the engine. I gave a real sigh of relief and a silent prayer for our young ordinary seaman. Now for all the paper work and explaining to people who only job is to try and find fault with my actions in trying to save the life of a young sailor.

When we arrived alongside at Lipari and commenced loading immediately the agent came onboard all smiles.

"Very good captain, very good please you give notice of readiness again."

"Sorry" I said

"I am not prepared to give notice again for legal reasons. The owners and charterers can sort that argument out among themselves"

The agent was a very happy man now any problems he might have regarding the ship he can blame me.

"We should complete loading tomorrow about noon and we will be ready for sea one hour later." I informed the agent. Weather permitting we should make the trip to Aberdeen in about ten days.

The following day we got away at 1400 for which I was most happy. I reckoned it would take us weather permitting at this time of the year, winter, about ten days to Aberdeen. The weather was dirty all the way home, constantly shipping seas fo'ard but not too heavy. All things considering we made a good trip until we got of the port. Because of the weather the pilot service was suspended which meant for ships of our size the port was shut. I called the harbour and asked permission to enter without a pilot. The big trawlers were all entering without a pilot. A pilot called me on the VHF and said.

"Captain I believe your going to enter without a pilot, That's ok but keep your speed up until your through the breakwater and then get it off as quickly as possible. I will board you at the turning basin."

I replied, "All understood I'll make my approach now if the entrance is clear."

"All clear captain, good luck" called the pilot.

As I entered between the break waters a big following sea started to build up. I thought if that breaks on the deck it will wash the mate over the side I think we had a little too much speed on. Slow ahead I shouted to the third mate as the engine slowed the big sea fell away as we cleared the breakwater inward. The pilot climbed onboard in the turning basin as planned. As he came onto the bridge and shook hands he enquired if I had been here before. I answered in the negative.

"Nice job, nice job captain I wondered if you would really attempt the entrance it is rather narrow for this size of ship in the present weather conditions."

"There is certainly a very nasty sea running out there in that wind."

It was only minutes to our berth and being all

fast fore and aft. I really felt relieved when I said to the young third mate. "Ring, Finished with Engines" the voyage was completed. The whole ship fell silent, the hum of the radars, the decca navigator the gyro compasses, radios and all the little alternators, converters and what have you all stopped as the third mate switched them all off. The chief reduced his engine room to one generator the silence through the ship was golden. As I came off the bridge all the usual shore people were waiting for me customs, agent, ship chandlers, emigration. The most important man among them was the agent with the ships mail. Among the ships official mail was our next orders. Similar to our last voyage. Load Emden for Sardinia but this time the discharging port would be Porto Vesme same cargo thence to Lipari to load same cargo again for Aberdeen when my leave would be due.

The mate Basil and I went ashore together just to have a look at the place. It looked grey and miserable with big stone buildings. We found a rather nice lounge bar where we could put our feet up and enjoy their bacardi. I told Basil I would have to go ashore in the morning to attend to the ships business namely 'note protest' and get my hair cut. The lounge bar was quite warm and hospitable, needless to say we sat on and had a great yarn about ships we served in and companies we had worked for. It was soon time to go, as we left the bar there seemed to me crowds of people about much the worst of wear for drink I saw what I could never get over and that was young men urinating against walls as they held their girl friends hand. I thought that was bad until I witnessed young girls urinating in doorways. With their big bare asses half out into the street. I had seen much in a lifetimes travel round the world but that beat all. The whole town seemed to me to be totally degenerate. It wasn't just one or two but quite a few.

Next day as I was getting my hair cut the barber asked me where I was from just to make conversation. I was also asked what I thought of Aberdeen. I told him of my experiences the previous evening. He said, "Ach man is that all they were doing?" Before sailing we were saddened to learn that the parents of the young seaman we landed ashore at Milazzo had to be flown to his bedside in Milazzo.

CHAPTER EIGHTEEN

DISCHARGING WOULD BE COMPLETED the following evening when we hoped to get away as soon as possible thereafter. That would be very good, as it would give us a daylight arrival at Emden. It would take about thirty hours to the Pilot station at the entrance to the Ems and then the run up the river we should make a daylight arrival at the Emden locks. It was important to get all the Pumice Stone discharged with little to clean out at sea. If we were caught cleaning holds at sea the Germans more than anyone else would heavily fine the ship and me on a charge of pollution. It was nearly 2200 in the evening of the following day that we eventually sailed. It was typical North Sea passage in winter. The sea was on our beam the whole way across to Emden and being in ballast we rolled really heavily. It was a pleasure to get the German pilot onboard and run up a nice smooth river to the locks and then to our berth. Loading commenced at once and was expected to finish the following day. The weather was so cold, wet and miserable that I didn't bother to venture ashore at all. I don't think anyone else did either. Everyone was looking forward to getting down to the Mediterranean to get the sun on their backs and a bit of heat into them.

Loading was completed the afternoon after we arrived and sailing took place one hour later. A few hours and we cleared the locks and disembarked the pilot at the Ems Pilot cutter. As soon as we established ourselves in the southbound shipping lane. I gave all my sailing cables to sparkey to send steaming time to Porto Vesme would be about nine days. In a couple of days we should be down by the Lizard and heading down to Gibraltar. As we crossed the Bay of Biscay the barometer commenced to drop and the cloud base lowered considerably with the wind strengthening all the time from the southwest. I knew we were in for a real bad storm. My fears were confirmed by the reports on our Navtex. (Our weather report recorder.) As we crossed the Bay of Biscay the weather got steadily worse. In bad weather, if a system does not commence to moderate by the third day you can be assured that the sea will become mountainous by that time.

We were now just west of Cape Finisterre in mountainous seas and storm force winds with no sign of the weather abating. Just off our port quarter was a small Danish ship known as a Ringkobber so called because that is were that class of ship is built. They are about 800 tons deadweight and trade throughout the world. This Ringkobber had lashed on her hatches a little motorcar. We wondered was it cargo or did it belong to her captain, maybe. The little ship was having a hell of a time in the storm. We couldn't help wondering how long the car was going to last on her deck before it would go overboard. We ourselves were 'hove too' with just making steerageway. When our Radio Officer received a Mayday Relay from the Large German container ship *Munchen* she was 47,000 tons. We were given to understand that she had gone down with all hands. That was so sad and also so frightening for all ships in the storm. She was too far away from us to be of any help. Our speed was down to bare steerageway, about three knots. It was another three days before we began to make any headway. We were abeam of Vigo before we really began to get going again. The little Danish ship with his car still on the hatches was still struggling to make headway. We still had five days steaming to Porto Vesme. Needless to say we eventually arrived there. It was a rather nasty approach to the entrance and the pilots would not take us alongside during the hours of darkness, which meant we had to anchor overnight.

Next morning the pilot was onboard early which meant we were all fast in the discharging berth by breakfast time. Port formalities were completed by 1000. That evening after tea the mate and I went for a walk. From the ship there was a long narrow road with no lights on it which lead up to the main road into town, which was very well lit. We went into a rather nice establishment sat down and ordered our usual bacardi and coke. On the other side of the bar a bunch of local lads were sitting, about a dozen or more of them Basil and I left the bar and headed back to the ship. The boys who were also in the bar passed us on the other side of the road. They were quite boisterous, we were walking rather slowly. I did notice the boys turning into the darkened road, which led, down to our ship. When we arrived at the darkened road it was very quiet which made me somewhat alarmed. There was nobody about, yet I knew these lads couldn't disappear into thin air. Suddenly they charged out of the bushes by the roadside and hit Basil who fell immediately to the road. Three of them jumped on me and dragged me into the bushes. I fought like hell as they tried to pull me down onto the roadside. As two fought with me the other tried to go through my pockets. Luckily a car turned into the road, which scared them. They stopped fighting and I could see Basil lying in the middle of the road. They jumped me again as I hit one of them suddenly they ran off as quickly as they had attacked us. When I got to my feet the mate had disappeared from the road. Not wanting to risk going down that road again on my own I made it to the main road and ran back to town and found a police station.

A big sign above the door CARABINIERI I knocked quite loudly on the door to no avail. Eventually somebody opened an upstairs window and stuck their head out and shouted something to me which I didn't' understand. Anyway I answered in English, and then I could hear big bolts moving on the door inside. Carabinieri open the door and beckoned me in. I tried to tell them what happened when obviously an officer of some rank who spoke good English commenced to question me. But what intrigued me more than anything was the carabinieris put a large table in the hallway opposite their hall doorway. On the table they put what to me was a bren gun (machine gun). Each time the door was knocked the Bren gun was manned. I thought it best to move out of the line of fire of anyone returning fire. I moved into someone's office. I could hear loud knocking at the door and suddenly above all else the voice of our chief officer who was looking for me could be heard. Anyway our ships agent arrived to take us back to the ship, with a police escort. On the way back down the darkened road just about where we were attacked, in the car headlights I spotted laying on the road our chief officers spectacles the car stopped and Basil recovered his glasses for which he was most grateful. I discovered later that my only loss was my local library ticket.

Next morning there was quite a buzz around the ship about the captain and the chief officer being attacked ashore. It was soon brought to my notice that many of our crew had been attacked last night. I went down to the crew accommodation to visit the boys only to find one so badly beaten that he really need hospital treatment. I sent the third officer the duty officer ashore to the stevedore's office to order our agent, police and an ambulance to the ship immediately. They all arrived eventually, the third officer travelled in the ambulance with the injured sailor to the hospital. The young seaman was terrified in case I left him behind in the hospital; he hated the place so much. I assured him when we sailed, with the doctor's permission I would take him back onboard and let him recuperate onboard. The carabinieris showed no real interest in our problem, they were more interested in our sailing date to get rid of us. I might say the feeling was mutual throughout the ship with respect to Sardinia. Thankfully sailing day did come a little sooner than expected, about six hours sooner. Everyone seemed to want rid of us including the stevedores. We got our young sailor onboard who was only suffering nasty bruising really. The ships business was soon attended too allowing the agent to get away as soon as possible. I went up to the bridge the pilot was already there and the chief officer already had the ship on stations for sailing. "Lets go pilot" I shouted, maybe it was my imagination but we seemed to get off the berth with some haste and disembark the pilot rather quickly at the pilot station. Another thirty-two hours and we should be arriving of Lipari again. I prayed to God this is a peaceful visit with no more sickness or anything else untoward.

As we were approaching the berth I couldn't help wondering if it would be the same agent as before. It would certainly be the same agency company. There he was standing on the quay waiting for us trying to see who the captain was. I gave him a wave, which he returned rather excitedly I thought. The crew soon had the gangway out and the usual entourage of officials came onboard. I soon dealt with them all the agent asked for a promise that we wouldn't run away again. "OK Mr agent I promise." The chief came into my cabin for permission to immobilize the engines for about twelve hours. I asked was it absolutely necessary and he said not really just routine maintenance. I said "Chief I'm sorry no not at this berth at this time of the year. The Minstral winds from the Gulf of Lyons are very strong at this time of the year and they could hit the berth suddenly. As you can see it is a very exposed berth. Not at this berth chief, sorry."

Another ship berthed alongside and commenced loading at another finger berth. During the night the duty officer called me because the ship was ranging a lot on the berth and the wind was getting much stronger. I told him to call the chief and get the engines on stand-by. Just after daylight I called the harbour master and informed him that the berth was too dangerous to lie at because of the bad weather. It was my decision to go to sea until the weather moderated. The chief asked for half an hour to warm the engine through if that was ok. Whilst the chief had his half hour the rest of us had a mug of coca. As soon as the chief was ready the mate sent all hands to stations. During the short time we were alongside the crew had been feeding an auld mongrel which sat at the bottom of the gangway all day waiting for food. He was still there as we were preparing for sea. I shouted through a loud hailer. "Don't let that bloody ould hound onboard". No sooner had I shouted my order that it run to the far edge of the quay and took a run and a leap between the dockside and us. It landed full square on the deck. (A ship can get into serious trouble for carrying an animal into a foreign country) At that one of our sailors lifted the dog swung it round his head and threw it over the quay were it landed on its ass. In seconds it was up on its feet and away up the quay yelping just as we were pulling clear of the berth.

I cabled the owners advising them of my actions and told them we would find a sheltered part of the coast and drift about until the weather improved when we would berth again and continue loading. The other ship at the other finger berth was in difficulty. He was being ordered off the berth by the port authorities for safety because of the bad weather. Unfortunately his engines were out of action and he couldn't comply with the harbour request. I was given to understand later that he caused considerable damage to the berth. Unfortunately as often happens in these cases the captain suffers by ending up in a court of law and jail. Which I understand was the outcome of this incident.

After steaming up and down with no change in the weather for nearly two days. I raised the owners on the MW radio and suggested they talk to the charterers. It would be better to come home with what cargo we did manage to load than waste money and time drifting about here. In a few hours they returned my call. They agreed and order us home with what cargo we had. The trip home would take about ten days always subject to the weather.

The weather moderated as we progressed through the Mediterranean Sea at Cap de Gata we were making 13 knots with the current in our favour. Once we cleared the straits and commenced our norwesterly course from Tarifa to Cap St. Vincent and started to feel the effect of the big winter swells one experiences of the Portuguese coast we nearly came to a standstill. All the way up to Ushant we rolled very heavily and as usual ran into thick fog at the Dowsing Bank in the North Sea. The watches were doubled up because of the fog, which in itself is very tiring for everyone. It wasn't too long before we had the Aberdeen pilot onboard. As we entered the harbour, I thought it was all rather different to the last time almost peaceful if not serene. The sea was just like glass with very little traffic (ships about) about. The crew soon had the gangway out, the ubiquitous officials were onboard rather quickly I thought. I was glad they were because I wanted to get packed and get away home. I had just spotted my relief on the quay with two of the crew helping him to get his gear onboard. The pressure of the voyage was already beginning to leave me.

CHAPTER NINETEEN

My wife was at the airport to meet me as usual. I was delighted to be home even though I knew most of the time would be the spent at meetings concerned with the wrapping up of my business. I would be glad to see the back of it all. After I had been at home a few days, the eggshell days as my wife referred to them as she gave me the entire official mail, which had arrived at home for me whilst I was away. There it was as usual the INLAND REVENUE on Her Majesty Service. I thought they wouldn't give up until they have my head on a platter. I couldn't believe it, from the Tax Commissioners themselves a final demand. They reckoned I owed them £1250 not bad I reckoned £1300. I was delighted I couldn't get to a phone quick enough to confirm with them that this was the lot as far as the present claim was concerned. A guy asked me to hold whilst he brought up my tax calculations I suppose on a computer screen.

"That was my total debt to date as shown."

"I suppose settlement would totally clear my indebtedness to Her Majesty," I suggested. I sent them a cheque by return of post. After I dropped the cheque into the post box I felt I was walking on air, just great my fight with the revenue was vindicated.

The winter is not a time when one can enjoy Ireland and yet I was not very interested in going abroad on holiday. I always feel I have spent enough time away from home. Whilst one can argue that it is possible to take your wife away on a holiday nevertheless it is nice to be able to spend time with family and friends also. A period of leave always seems to go very quickly and when ones leave is up you just wonder were it went to.

The captain on one of our ships the *Ashington* had to be relieved at Odda in Norway and as my leave was nearly up I had to go and relieve him. This entailed an awful journey especially when carrying full sea going gear. At that time I was able to get a flight direct from Belfast to Bergen. I had been given a list of buses and ferries, which I had to catch. Each within minutes of the other leaving. From the airport I got a bus into Bergen and a Taxi to the underground bus station in the centre of town. There to catch the bus over the mountains. This bus was fitted with snow chains but it still slid around the mountain roads, which were all right provided one, didn't look out the window into the ravine below. Change to a ferry to cross the fiord then another bus up a mountain and down the other side to another fiord. Then another ferry, which was no larger than an overgrown motor cruiser except that it had a terrific turn of speed. On board was an Arabic family complete by wearing shadoors. (Traditional black Shia cloak). Four women and a couple of little boys and myself. They did look somewhat out of place up there in Norway. It was getting very dark; the next place we called at was just a jetty with a hut on it and a bit of a shelter at the bus stop. The ferry sped away and when it was out of sight and earshot the whole place took on a rather eerie atmosphere about it. I could see one wee light miles away along the fiord. It was far enough away to convince me that I certainly couldn't walk it and most certainly not with all my gear.

I began to wonder to they have wolves in Norway. Maybe something will eat me before morning. God, what a place to be left standing. A car drew up at the bus stop and a young couple got out and sat down in the bus shelter. I went over to them and asked about the bus, which is supposed to stop here for Odda. They assured me a bus would come, sometime. A car drew up at the stop and the young couple got into it. Once again I stood in the dark wondering when the phantom bus might show up. At last the bus arrived and the driver helped me with my gear. I gave him my ticket and just hopped I was on the correct bus. I felt sure there wouldn't be too many buses about in these parts. Eventually it called into a big car park, which I recognised as Odda. As I came down the bus steps the agent who was waiting for me stepped forward and shook hands. I knew him from trips in the past to Odda. He and I got into his car as he put all my gear on the back seat. The agent then run me round the dockside to my ship and helped me up the gangway with my gear. Very kind of him indeed, I offered him a beer, which he declined. He said, "until tomorrow captain."

"Ok then, tomorrow thanks".

He left the ship in a hurry. Just as I was taking my coat off the second mate called at my cabin and told me that a nice hot meal had been kept for me in the hot press, just for me joining this evening. I just thought what a thoughtful crew I have inherited.

Odda as a town was quite interesting but I never really liked it for some reason. It was like living in a bucket if you wanted to see out one always had to look up. It was at the head of a fiord from which very steep mountains ascended. Actually I found it to be a bit claustrophobic, after about three days in the place I always felt a little nauseated. Or maybe it was because the dockside to which the ship tied up was so close to the hills especially the stern end where the accommodation block was. Up the hill side overlooking the ship was a small block of flats. The bay window of one, which the local female custom officer owned, the one closest to the ship. It was alleged that she never missed a trick from that window. A very good Polish friend of mine called Jarofwhisky, was caught by her doing a little business which cost him a small fortunate in fines. But being a resourceful sort of guy he went back down to his ship and opened his wee business again to earn the cash to pay his fines. When his ship sailed everyone in the town was very happy including Jarofwhisky.

There was a Hotel near the dockside, which supported a nice lounge bar. Unfortunately it would have been cheaper to buy a brewery in England that to try and buy a beer in Norway. I think that observation would be true for the whole of Scandinavia. One could take a very long walk up a very steep hill to see a typical Norwegian lake. When you would arrive at the top of the hill you would pay anything for a beer. The lake in question is reputed to be the highest lake in Norway.

Our sailing time was 1800 tomorrow night for Workington to load coal for St. Nazaire. It was my intention to go down the leads (Inside route on the Norwegian Coast) and drop our pilot at Coppervik. That is exactly what we did. All went well until we were almost at the Pentland Firth in a force 8 Gale that was expected to come away to force 9 gusting 10. The chief wanted to stop for at least twelve hours. He had trouble with the fuel valves on the main engine, which must be changed.

"Keep her going until Scapa Flow can you do that? Then I will anchor and you can have as long as you like with your engine," He agreed. We anchored rather close the sunken second world war battleship *Royal Oak* sixteen hours after anchoring the chief was ready to proceed.

It didn't take too long to get the anchor up and

get underway. To our advantage the tide was westerly as we entered the Pentland Firth, which meant the passage through the Firth was very good. In about forty-eight hours and we should be tied up at Workington. A couple of days alongside waiting for tides, loading etc and we should be away again bound for St. Nazaire. Loading went very well at Workington we were soon out into the Solway Firth again and heading south. The weather as usual was dirty and expected to get much worse as we headed south to the Scilly Isles with the intention of heading over the to 'Ushant' on the French Coast. We were about nine miles NNE from the 'Seven Stones Light' when I thought I could smell something burning. At this time I was sitting in the officer's smoke room watching television everywhere seemed clear when I went out of the smoke room to sniff the atmosphere, the smell had gone away. Naturally I thought it was my imagination. I went back into the smokeroom to continue watching the television. I had just sat down when an AB (a sailor, senior rating) shouting, "The engineroom is on fire" I dashed up to the bridge and as I did so I could hear the alarm bells ringing. The mate was on watch luckily we had a very capable young mate. He reported the ship closed up on fire stations. I felt like a bloody fool being last to arrive on the bridge not having heard the alarm. Reports started coming into the bridge. It would seem that the funnel packing and insulation had burst into flames for some reason and was falling blazing onto the generator flat.

The weather was really bad by this time, blowing force nine from the westward with a big sea running. We were in the southbound shipping lane to the Scillys, not a good place to be in a disabled ship. We sealed the engineroom but that asphyxiated the generators with associated loss of power. It was imperative to maintain power if at all possible. I had sparks attend the radios but unfortunately he was from an agency for the employment of Radio Officers. All our permanent radio officers having been made redundant. The government only required a radio officer to be carried on certain voyages and this was one of them. The captains are now expected to be the radio officer. This was one time when all these cuts in manning caused considerable danger to a ship. Our radio officer had just joined the ship in Workington before sailing and wasn't fully conversant with the ships radios. I went on the VHF and sent a PAN message. (A PAN message is a warning to all ships of a ship in trouble but not in such trouble as requiring urgent help if that was the case an SOS would be sent.) Lands End coastguard replied asking me how bad was the situation. I told them very bad but that my crew were fitting the fire in the engineroom. At this stage I did not want to abandon my ship I thought my crew would beat the fire. The coastguard put two helicopters from 'Culdrose' on standby in case I wanted to abandon. Ship. Had the weather been better I may well have been tempted to do so but the weather was wild and we were rolling very heavily but not violently. I considered fighting the fire and saving the ship rather that getting out of the ship the lesser of two evils at present. The chief engineer and the chief officer (that is the mate) felt they could contain it and eventually extinguish it. I advised the coastguard of my intention to try and reach Penzance Bay a safe anchorage and if they would keep the emergency services on stand by until I did so.

The crew managed to control the fire until we arrived in the bay and found a sheltered anchorage. The chief engineer managed to remove all the packing from the funnel when we anchored. In the funnel was a thermal oil tank, which had a broken gauge. It seemed to be broken for sometime which caused all the packing to be soaked in oil. The heat in the funnel caused the whole lot to ignite the result being a severe fire. At breakfast the ships company were watching SW Television when much to everyone's delight SW Television News paid the whole ship especially myself great accolades. They referred to the brave captain and crew (The television announcers words not mine) of the British ship *Ashington* fighting to save their blazing ship in last nights severe storm whilst two Royal Navy helicopters at 'Culdrose' stood by to evacuate the crew if necessary.

I was rather concerned about that broadcast because no doubt some wives would hear it and become somewhat alarmed. I rang personnel in our office put them in the picture and requested them to advise the wives of all hands that there was nothing to worry about. Unfortunately a local person in Cornwall, friends of one of our engineers from Tyneside rang to tell them what they had heard on the news. The wife in question immediately rang my wife to tell her. However, my wife Sheelagh is a lady of very quiet disposition, a person who was not prone to panic, she told the wife in question. "The officers and crew would know what they were doing so there would be nothing to worry about. Forget about it all until you hear something official".

On arrival at St. Nazaire a French maritime investigation team came onboard to go through the log books and interview the crew. I thought this was all a bit out of order. We were a British ship registered in the Isle of Man and didn't need the French to investigate us. Not so the French view of events, they said we had a very serious incident at sea and a French port was the first port of call after the incident and so they would investigate the matter. On reflection I suppose they where correct. I must say they were very through indeed and in some ways I was very pleased that they were.

The agent was most helpful, what I would describe as a young girl a very lovely young girl. She was just wearing a cotton dress but looked very beautiful. I always thought that about continental girls no matter what they wore they always look smart. I think it had something to do with deportment. She took me ashore to her office so that I could telephone my office and report the matter in detail to them. After we sailed on passage down the Loire the remainder of the funnel packing burst into flames again. This time the crew had the fire out in minutes. The pilot didn't even know that we had had a fire onboard, which was just as well. One never knows what sort of panic he might have caused among the shore authorities.

CHAPTER TWENTY

We had orders to proceed to Le Harve and load a cargo of coal for Grangemouth, which we did after Grangemouth we proceeded to Workington to load another cargo of coal for St Nazaire. Unfortunately when entering the locks at Workington we had engine trouble in the locks. The engines were being controlled from the bridge when the pneumatic bridge control jammed. If the control were moved forward to make the engine go ahead the reverse would take place. The pilot called for a kick of full ahead instead what he got was a kick full astern. The ship came astern and hit the knuckle on the lock gate with such force I was knocked off my feet. The stern of the ship was set in by about one foot, which was considerable damage requiring a trip to the to the Tyne for repairs.

I had been appointed permanent master of the *Donnington*, which at the time was one of the largest ships in the fleet and one of the newest. I was very pleased to get my own ship instead of continually transferring from one ship to another. The problem is, in any shipping company, if your long enough in command of the same ship you begin to feel you own it. I eventually ended up in command of the *Donnington* from February 1980 until August 1992 twelve years. I did from time to time, short periods relieving on other ships but substantially I served in the *Donnington,* she was recognised in the fleet as Captain Potts ship. On reflection it was a good twelve years. During that period I met many wonderful people both ashore and afloat. On long passages and on long periods at anchor I needed a hobby because I was always the type of guy who needed to keep his brain active.

I read law as an external student with London University through Wolsey Hall, Oxford that I thoroughly enjoyed. When it came to the final examinations Stephenson & Clarke the owners wrote to the examination board of London University and explained to them that I couldn't' be relieved in time to sit my examinations in June. The university very kindly allowed me to sit my examinations in London in the examination rooms in Euston Square with the referrals from the June examinations. On the condition that if I failed a paper I would have to sit the whole examination again and not the one paper. Through my lack of a good schooling as a boy I had a poor knowledge of history. Anyway that is my excuse for failing the paper 'The English Legal System' I had no intention of trying to make a career in the legal profession so I hadn't the incentive to start to it all over again. The knowledge I gleaned from my legal studies stayed me in good stead for the rest of my life.

I took my youngest son Michael to sea with me

M.V. DONNINGTON
Stephen Clarke Shipping
Ltd., Displacement
Tonnage 15,500 Tons

in the *Donnington* a few times, which he enjoyed immensely. One of our trips together was to Casablanca were we had about a week in port, which we made the best of. The ship chandler took us both on sightseeing trips to many parts of the town which we may not have been able to see otherwise, unless with a guide. The better residential areas in Casablanca are really beautiful especially the flowers in bloom in the gardens of peoples homes. In the French shopping areas there are many nice street cafes, which we made great, use of. Just sitting by a pavement café watching the style go by was most enjoyable. One evening two young girls passed us by holding hands, one totally covered in a Shador and her friend in a tight sweater with her boobs well supported and a skirt on hardly as deep as my belt. Michael I don't think ever forgot them. It was always a golden rule of mine to keep well clear of shady areas in the world. I always believed in the old saying '*Never trouble, trouble until trouble troubles you*'. Great rules no doubt but I wanted Michael to see the world as it is not as we think it is. The question in my mind was do I take him into the 'casba' or not. Yes, he is a big boy he can look after his oul da now. We're only going to the 'casba' not a 'knocking shop'. I had taken my older son to 'funny' London nightclubs in his younger days. So that was it, I decided, we would explore the 'casba' together so of we went. Typical when you came out of it again you felt as though you had escaped from somewhere. Anyway it was worth it Michael bought a really lovely leather jacket in it, which he got for about £40. Considering the haggling price started at £120 I think he did very well. It took a couple of days to get it down to that price. After the first visit to the 'casba' nothing would do Michael but we should go again. (Michael visited Fez when at university and saw the suffering of the children who had to dive into vats of dye used to dye the animal skins to be made into leather. It was children who dyed the leather. That I think was the end for Michael with Moroccan leather goods. The lovely leather jacket was never seen again).

Upon completion of discharge and the cleaning of the holds we moved to the loading berth and loaded a cargo of phosphates for Helsingborg. A really awful cargo to load because of the dirt it creates. The ship was totally covered in a cloud of phosphate dust, which gets into ones eyes and every orifice of the body. Thankfully it does not take too long to load. On completion of loading I am expected to go along to the offices on the quay and sign for the cargo together with all bills pertaining to my vessel. After signing I am given a payment for my efforts of a few hundred Dirhams the local currency which is totally useless outside Morocco. Upon returning to my ship the local mandatory Moroccan nightwatch man is always at the top of the gangway bowing and saluting me as I come onboard. It is always he I give the Dirhams to. You then go through the ritual of him grabbing your hand and kissing it. A few hundred Dirhams is an awful lot of money to these guys. It is embarrassing to see their show of gratitude.

As usual we rolled our way north and shipped plenty of water on deck crossing the Bay of Biscay. As we passed the Skaw into the Baltic the usual Fog banks appeared which make life rather difficult. People ashore think that looking at radar set is like watching the television.

Everything can be seen clearly on the screen. Not so, all the targets have to be plotted so that their courses and speeds can be ascertained and avoided if necessary. To do that for four solid hours is most strenuous. In a two-watch ship working six hours on and six hours off it is very much worse. A merchant ship is not like a warship with all kinds of bodies on the bridge or in special plotting rooms plotting the ship. The merchant ship just has the master and the officer of the watch on the bridge plotting and navigating the ship.

Once passed the Skaw and into the Baltic certain routes must be adhered too. This is because of mine fields and numerous obstructions on the seabed from the Second World War, which makes anchoring in certain areas dangerous to say the least. There are very many active defence minefields on the Swedish coast, which must also be treated with the highest respect. Also difficult channels with restricted water such as the Drogden Channel. The Aland Archipelago is all difficult areas for navigators in the Baltic especially in fog. It also means many days and nights on the bridge for the master of a ship.

To let Michael see part of Denmark, as we were so near to it, we took the ferry across to Ellsinore to the market. On the return trip the clink of bottles in tripper's bags was like listening to the 'Bells of St Mary's.' We found a very nice restaurant called the Lord Nelson in which we had a black and white steak. It really was served half black and half white. All very nice but when the bill came we were convinced that we were really the new owners of the establishment. The only other tourist attraction I could find was the Castle of Helsingborg, which had hundreds of steps up to it from the road to the castle itself. I took one look at the steps and gave it a miss. I would have had a heart attack if I had attempted that climb. Michael was not that keen to visit the castle that he would have left me sitting waiting for him to return

When we did eventually return back onboard the chief officer met us on the gangway only to advise me that one of the stewards had been causing very considerable trouble. I tried to talk some sense into this young man, all to no avail. I called for police help and had him arrested. He spent the night in jail and felt rather sorry for himself upon his return to the ship next day. He was very lucky that he wasn't sacked from the ship on arrival back in the UK. He was one of the stewards to be made redundant in the reorganisation of crew manning. Had he been sacked he would have lost his redundancy money. His conduct was such that criminal charges under the Merchant Shipping Acts might well have been laid before him. Upon reflection he was a very lucky man and he knew it.

Upon completion of discharge we proceeded round the Swedish coast and up to the head of the Gulf of Bothina to a little port called Skelleftea. There was nothing in the place except a small loading plant for Ore Pellets, which was our cargo for Immingham. It was quiet and had that serenity about it often associated with Swedish forests and lakes. I walked for miles and sat on a bench for hours just absorbing the stillness and thinking of home and my years ashore. At least if nothing else I got to know my family during their teen years whilst ashore. Though I missed their junior years, which can never be recaptured. The loss of those years reflected my family relationships in later years. Years, which were sadly missed, as I grew older and the family dispersed about England.

The next day we sailed down the Gulf of Bothnia and through the Aland Islands, which as mentioned before is a nasty little archipelago especially in fog, which is what happened to us. Loaded we were too deep to go out of the Baltic up through the Drogden channel we had to use the Belts which was a great education for Michael. Eventually we were across the North Sea rolling our guts out due to the heavy Iron ore cargo low down in the bottom of the ship. On arrival at Immingham I was relieved as I had some leave due. Michael and I travelled home together, he couldn't wait to get home and relate the stories of his voyage to his friends.

An emergency cropped up in the company onboard one of our smaller ships the *Jade*. The captain of the ship took seriously ill and had to be relieved in Cork as soon as possible. My leave was nearly up so I was sent down to Cork to relieve him. Unfortunately the man died a few weeks later. Cork was a place I had never been to. The ship was discharging bags of cement and drawn up alongside the ship to receive the cargo were numerous donkeys and carts. In this day and age I was astonished at such a mode of transport still in use and in such numbers. My visit to cork was most interesting. I must say I was astonished to see so many maids of doubtful charm trying to get onboard the ship at night usually to try and beg a meal. Or anything else that was going free. Many of these ladies lived in the dockside containers left lying about the docks. I would like to think that was all in the past since the Republic reaped the benefit of the Common Market.

We sailed for Plymouth to load cement for Magheramorne near Larne. When the customs came onboard at Plymouth they said "Your loading for Larne captain"

I replied. "No I am loading for Magheramorne"

"In that case your entitled to a bond issue, captain" (If a ship is just calling in the United Kingdom from foreign and is sailing for foreign again the crew are entitled to a duty free issue after a specific number of days in a UK port It is either ten or twelve days. I just can't remember). Obviously the custom officers knowledge of geography left much to be desired.

We sailed from Magheramorne to Llanddulas to load Lime Stone for Brunsbuttle on the Elbe.

Not having been to Llanddulus before which is only a finger jetty running out from the North Wales coast into sea. The company sent another captain who was well versed in running to Llanddulus to act as pilot. My interest was to get to Brunsbuttle as quickly as possible because I was leaving this ship there and rejoining my own ship at Rouen. My orders were to load a full cargo of grain at Rouen for Casablanca.

On arrival at Brunsbuttle I left the *Jade* and travelled to Hamburg where I spent the night in a hotel. To get to Rouen it was necessary to fly to Paris from Hamburg and there take a train to Rouen, this I did. On arrival at Charles de Gaul airport I enquired at the information desk as to how I could get into Paris. The lady at the desk suggested I share a taxi into the city, she suggested I ask the guy beside me if he would like to do so. Having overheard the conversation with the lady at the desk the guy turned to me and asked if he could travel into Paris with me. I agreed and moved off towards the taxi ranks. He seemed to have difficulty walking so I offered to help him with his gear for which he was very pleased. As we got into the taxi and moved off I enquired of him if he was all right.

He had had an operation on his foot and also six foot of his intestine removed due to cancer. In the course of conversation it transpired that he was going to join a ship at Le Harve. He was in fact the captain of one of the United States Line ships. I understood the officers of the American Merchant Marine were well paid but from his information they seemed to be totally bereft of any social benefits. Certainly a man in such poor health would just not be allowed to sail in a British ship let alone command it. I must say I felt at the time, proud to be serving in the British Merchant Navy and I told him so. He told me he had heard about the conditions of service in the British Merchant Navy but he often wondered if it was true or not, I was the first person he had ever met who could confirm the social benefits enjoyed by British seamen. On arrival in Paris at the railway station we said our good byes to each other and went our separate ways to our trains.

I arrived onboard only to be advised by the agent and the custom officers to be very careful at our present berth because there had been an awful lot of problems with people slipping onboard at night and stealing anything they could get their hands on. It would be unlikely to have any trouble that night. A large Bore was expected on the river, which meant the crew would be on stations all night until the Bore passed. Everyone onboard was warned about thieving in French ports and hence strongly advised to keep their cabin doors locked especially at night. The third engineer had travelled by train all the way from the

Le Havre ferry terminal to Rouen with a large tape recorder on his knees he thought that would be the safest way to carry it. Of course he ignored the instructions given to him about cabin safety when he joined the ship and so the tape recorder disappeared from the third engineers cabin that night never to be seen again.

Eventually we sailed down what is a very winding, twisty, river the, Seine and into the English Channel. The weather was pleasant throughout the passage south. All during this time the second officer who had his wife with him continuously complained of pains in his stomach. About three days from Casablanca I examined him. Up to that time he just refused to have me look at him, continuously saying there is nothing really wrong with me. When he did condescend to have me examine him I came to the conclusion that he was suffering from appendicitis. This I told his wife who immediately told me in no uncertain terms that I was talking nonsense. She said, "She knew her husband, he was always regular everyday and all he needed was a good laxative," I told her "under no circumstances would he be given a laxative of any description. He would receive only sips of Luke warm water" I couldn't quite make up my mind whether to land him in Gibraltar or continue on with him to Casablanca. I was afraid of peritonitis setting in. I decided to continue the voyage and land him in Casablanca. Every time I examined him she was leaning over me trying to get me to change my opinion, telling me he only needs a laxative. I must say she was becoming very annoying.

A radio message was sent to Casablanca advising them that I had an emergency medical case onboard, which I think helped us to get a berth on arrival. I gave my medical letter for the hospital to the agent to deliver personally to the hospital, as I was afraid it might be tampered with. Having advised his wife of my intention to land her husband in hospital I offered to arrange for her to be repatriated or get accommodation for her in Casablanca whilst her husband was in hospital. What ever she choose it would be for her expense but that I would advise the British Consulate of her predicament who I'm sure would look after her. It so happened that the British Consulate turned out to be a lady who just could not do enough for the well being of the second officer's wife. She insisted on finding accommodation for the wife and not to bother my agent. I wrote to her later and thanked her so much for all her help and kindness. Sometime later I was told just how much she really did look after our second officers wife.

After discharging our grain cargo we moved to the phosphate berth and loaded a full cargo of phosphates for Landskrona.

CHAPTER TWENTY ONE

ON OUR PASSAGE NORTH as we were passing Cape St. Vincent I was working in the chartroom when I heard a bit of a commotion on the deck outside. I looked up from my work and there in the wheelhouse stood one of our AB's with what looked like a monkey or some black filthy aberration. Said the AB. "I found him in the funnel" I knew it, a bloody stowaway, that's all we need. When loading phosphate the cloud of phosphate dust, which covers the whole, ship in phenomenal. The dust cloud reduces visibility to a few feet at times making it easy for stowaways to slip onboard and hide in the various nooks and crannies onboard a ship.

We had Arab ratings in the engineroom. I told the officer of the watch to have an engineroom rating sent to the bridge to act as an interpreter. Having explained what I wanted the rating to do he held up his hands and said. "Ah captain, captain. I can't speak wat dis man say. I from Yemen he Africa".

Says the third mate "I think he is trying to tell us he doesn't speak his dialect."

"Is that a fact?" I said to no one in particular. I turned to the 3rd Officer and told him to ring the chief officer and tell him he is wanted on the bridge. As soon as the chief officer appeared on the bridge I had a discussion with him as to what we should do with our stowaway. "Great" said he.

"Wonderful, I'll turn him too and he can replace the steward we lost in the organisation of the catering department. He can keep all the public rooms and alleyways clean. Captain I suggest we keep him in the hospital clear of everyone until such times as we get to know him. He will also have his own bathroom and loo clear of the crew just incase of diseases he may be carrying."

I said to the chief officer. "Good thinking, get him cleaned up, showered etc and get the motorman to try again to understand what he is trying to say. Main thing is to make him understand that as long as he is here he will work. Just so long as he obeys his orders he will be safe and looked after".

"Marcus, it is when we get into port we will have real trouble with this guy. He has no papers so he will not be allowed to land. We will be responsible for his custody. If he gets ashore the ship and myself will be very heavily fined. I will do everything possible to have him taken ashore and locked up whilst we are in port but not every port will do that". I advised the company of our situation and also the agents at Landskrona. My cable to the authorities ashore made it quite clear that there were no facilities onboard to detain our stowaway. He should be detained ashore if necessary. Either way it was going to be a costly exercise with this nonsense at every port.

When the agent and the various authorities came onboard it was made clear to me he, the stowaway was my responsibility whilst the ship was in Swedish waters. The agent was in touch with the Moroccan Embassy in Stockholm and everything possible was being done to have him repatriated. In the meantime I can keep him or have him locked up ashore whilst we are in port. I suggested he be kept in custody until we sailed. In the meantime an official from the Swedish immigration service paid me a visit. I was examined, cross-examined and latterly brain washed to the extent I was becoming a very annoyed captain. The Swedes were more interested in how I had been treating this guy than anything else. The questions I was asked I told them the German Gestapo wouldn't have the cheek to ask that. I refused to answer any more questions until I had advice from the British Consulate. They then apologised for causing me trouble and left the ship.

The next morning I had the agent send a car for me to take me up to his office to use the phone. I phoned the company and told them what the situation was. They advised me they would back me one hundred per-cent in any action I took to keep my stowaway in custody ashore or afloat. "The P&I Club (Is a mutual insurance club which shipowners join to look after their problems in foreign ports.

Unfortunately, It is not necessarily in the interests of the P&I Club to look after the interests of the master). Had everything in hand. Just be guided by their representatives, Captain." When I put down the phone I thought long and hard about what was said to me on the phone. I had considerable experience with different owners P&I Clubs when I was running the Potts Line with chartered ships. I regret to say many of the people I had to deal with from P&I clubs left much to be desired. They lacked the ability to see the bigger picture. Like two lawyers in a court of law playing with the legal niceties of a case whereas two country men would spit on their hands, clap them together and shake and the whole problem would have been sorted.

Our next port of call was Gdynia to load a full cargo of coal for the Power Station at Kiel this was just a short trip, only twenty hours steaming. By this time we had christened our stowaway Ali who seemed to think that was funny. When Ali learned we were bound for a communist port he became quite frightened. Some of the boys teased him mercilessly using sign language. I was able to get him to understand that if he were good I would not put him ashore in jail but allow him to stay on the ship. I told him if he went off the ship and the Poles caught him God knows what might happen to him. (I thought to myself God knows what might happen to me?) It was then he told me he liked the jail at Landskrona. Apparently it was at the top of a very high building in Landskrona where he had a panoramic view over the city.

On arrival at Gdynia the usual gang of officials arrived onboard. There are usually so many of these people visit the ship in Polish ports that I do not allow them in my accommodation. I use the saloon to conduct the ships business in. They all look for their carton of cigarettes and a bottle of whisky. There is usually about ten or twelve of these guys and before I gave them any 'handouts' I enquired as to what they were going to do about him pointing at our stowaway. They could see their 'goodies' sitting on the saloon sideboard. 'We will leave him on the ship captain, but it will be a heavy fine if he leaves the ship.' God, I thought in my old age I'm really getting soft. But how could one put a wee fella like Ali who is just a silly wee boy in a communist jail.

We were soon loaded and in a few hours were alongside the power station in Kiel. Because I had a stowaway onboard I think the German army was sent onboard. When I came off the bridge to go to my cabin I could hardly get passed them all to get to my cabin. On completion of the ships business the Immigration Police gave me quite a lecture. If Ali could get ashore and was picked up ashore by the Police he was entitled to apply for an entrance permit. He could leave Germany and as long as he came back within two years his original application was valid. However, if he couldn't get ashore in the first place he couldn't make an application to enter the country.

Therefore it was imperative that he didn't get off the bloody ship. I said to them "If it is so important to you to keep him out of your country you had better lock him up." This they refused to do as he would be deemed to have been taken into the country and they didn't want that. "Right then I will keep him best I can." They did agree to keep a watch on the ship and there always seemed to be one of them within hailing distance from the ship if we needed help.

Young Ali wasn't too happy when we told him we were going back to Poland. We had been ordered back to Gdynia to load coal for Cork. As soon as we completed discharge in Kiel we sailed for Gydnia. At least we didn't have to worry too much about cleaning holds for the next cargo. As soon as we loaded I sailed and this time it was my intention as usual to go out from the Baltic up through the Great Belt and round the Skaw into the North Sea.

When we eventually arrived at Cork the authorities boarded including the Police. I made it very clear to the Garda Siochana (Irish Police) that I had no means of restraining anyone onboard the ship. They were most insistent that I try. I had the bos'un screw down the dogs on the hospital ports using a marlin spike. The chief officer checked these for security. The Police sent one of their men down to the ship at meal times to let Ali out from the hospital to have his meals which time the Police would join him. The following morning Ali was away, he had escaped. Unfortunately for him the Garda who had help secure him in the ships hospital was the very Garda who spotted Ali in a Hotel car park. He immediately gave chase and caught him. He was back to the ship within minutes of us learning he was gone. The Garda by this time had summoned assistance; three of them accompanied Ali up the gangway. The officer with them was all smiles as he tried to hand him over to me. I refused to accept him he was now in their custody and they could do what they liked with him. In the end we came to an amicable settlement. The guards would keep him in the Brandywell Jail until I was ready for sea. I would then accept him back onboard and take him to sea with me. That was agreed and everyone was saved a lot of money. He was in the jail and so a lot of paper work was going to be involved with Ali's custody. I told the agent I wanted an official interpreter involved in the morning when I came to settle all the paper work. This was done, a rather nice young lady who was the lady who always acted as the official interpreter for the skippers of Spanish trawlers when they were arrested for illegal fishing in Irish waters. It just so happened that the lady interpreter also spoke fluent Arabic.

That evening she had to come down to the ship to get me to sign some papers. Most of the cargo had been discharged and so we were very light in the water and sitting high out of the water with the gangway ever so steep. She refused to attempt to climb the gangway so I went down to her car to do the signing.

As I got into her car she looked at me, so excited and said J..e..s..u..s captain what a big ship. (God I thought to myself you could only hear that in Ireland). The chief officer was repairing some damaged bunker tanks with plastic steel so sailing would be delayed until about breakfast time, perhaps a little later.

Upon sailing our orders were to load in Aughinish a full cargo of Bulk Aluminium for Blyth. It is only eighteen hours steaming to Aughinish and a little longer loading with their modern loading plant. I had decided to go to Blyth north about a decision I would live to regret. From Shannon to Cape Wrath the weather was very good. On arrival at Cape Wrath the bombing range was in use by Tornados of the Royal Air Force, the guard ship asked us to pass a little further to seaward. All hands were on deck watching the performance of the aircraft, real boys own stuff. The weather report for the North Sea wasn't very good if anything it was very bad and expected to get worse. A very large Norwegian bulkcarrier overhauled us. She was on passage from Glensander to the Medway with a cargo of quarrystone. During the afternoon we passed her going the other way. She advised us that the weather round by Duncansby Head was very bad and she had sustained damage she was looking for some shelter to carry out repairs. We wished her well and hope we wouldn't have any trouble. I thought that was a rather sudden change in the weather.

That night whilst passing the Firth of Fourth the chief officer was on watch. He called me to the bridge, looking a very worried man. He said "Captain I think we have serious trouble fo'ard. Watch those big seas breaking over the bow. She is not lifting her head to the sea. Each time she buries her head in a sea, she does not lift her head clear easily, she is struggling to clear the water fo'ard." I stood and watched for a while. "Yes I think your, right" by this time I had gone out unto the bridge wing and above the howling of the wind I could hear a lot of noise like something metal thrashing about. Right, I'm going into the Forth to find a sheltered spot to anchor and examine her for'ard. I don't like the noise up there. Advise the chief of my intentions he will have to change over to diesel in about thirty minutes. As we got further into the Firth of Fourth and obtained more shelter the Chief Officer and the Bo'sun went fo'ard to examine the damage best they could.

"Well mate, what have you got to tell me?" I said to him as he stepped onto the bridge. He reported "It looks very serious you can see for yourself now, in the calmer water she is well down by the head. We have lost an anchor and it looks like the loose cable from the hawse pipe has been thrashing about and has split the coaming of the scuttle into the rope locker foa'rd, opening it to the sea. The ship is totally flooded fro'ard in which case the bowthruster motor and everyother electrical appliance will be underwater and therefore knackered." "I told the mate to contact port control and ask for an anchorage. I know the anchorages here are all designated" In the meantime I'll disturb our engineering superintendent and give him the news of our damage. When we arrived at our anchorage daylight was breaking which had the makings of a nice day about it. I had the hatches all opened just to examine the cargo. At the hatch joints there was evidence of dampness but no real damage otherwise. The chain lockers, paint lockers, bos'un stores, motor rooms were all flooded. The rope locker looked as though a giant of sorts had been in the store just tangling and mixing all the ropes both wire and hemp together with fenders and all the other odds and ends. The damage was just unbelievable. Obviously we were going to have to get large industrial heaters onboard to dry the whole place out. Electricians would also be needed to repair the entire electrical fittings etc. The company's superintendents never fail in getting a ship repaired and underway again as quickly as possible. The shore staff will soon get it all sorted. One thing I must do is get customs clearance coming from Southern Ireland If the company hasn't already done so.

Sure enough about smoko time a launch came alongside with all kinds of bodies onboard including custom officers and our engineer superintendents and the lad from our agency department. As usual no time was wasted, a barge was also soon alongside with four large industrial heaters and a generator together with some shore guys to run it all. In just under four days all repairs were completed the anchor was aweigh and

I was underway down the Firth of Forth bound for Blyth. I did my own piloting in that part of the world and having decided it would be unwise to use the bowthruster so soon after our problems I decide to order a tug for berthing.

My next trip was Murmansk in Northern Russia to load fertilizer for Hamburg. The flooding had caused problems with our voyage planning overall. The delay caused by the flooding meant our possible spread of lay days was being shortened. I was asked could I get to Murmansk within the proposed time allowed. I could but not by going up the Norwegian Coast by the out side route it would it take a lot of luck and no swell. I could go up the leads, which would be expensive in terms of pilot fees. A message came through to the ship do what you deem necessary but get there. Right I'll go up the leads and I'll book my pilots now myself. I rang Coppervik and gave them my ETA telling them I needed pilots all the way to

Honningsvaag at the North Cape. Everything was set up for the voyage; I had a yarn with the chief engineer on the necessity of making a quick passage.

We did spend a little extra time alongside at Blyth to give the chief officer a chance to get his holds cleaned. The Russians can be rather pedantic about these matters sometimes. It would take about twenty-seven hours to Coppervik and about three days to Honningsvaag and another twelve hours Murmansk. Yes we should do it, just! Our passage across to

Coppervik, the pilot station on the Norwegian Coast was very good. The pilot said to me as we shook hands "It is so seldom that we see a British ship in the leads this must be a special occasion."

I replied. "It is not a special occasion but I am in a hurry because of my lay days. By the way pilot I trust you don't expect me to stay on the bridge throughout the whole passage through the leads." He looked surprised and assured me it was quite ok if I turned in.

He looked at me again and said, "The only ships we see up here now are Russian ships. Their captains all sleep. Except when they have phoney breakdowns, it is then the sketchpads appear and the officers all make sketches of the coastline. It is up to you captain what you do so long there is always an officer on the bridge."

There are only two places when it is necessary to leave the leads and go out to sea at each place it is only for a few hours. People from all over the world pay a lot of money to do what we are doing. This is a very popular voyage for tourists especially those tourists making the voyage on the Norwegian coastal steamers. I doubt if the very large cruise liners make the passage all the way through the leads. I think it is a case of visiting certain more picturesque fjords rather than covering the whole coastline as we were doing at present the scenery is just quite stunning. Just so long your not the navigator on watch looking over the side. The rocks seem to be just right alongside with a couple of feet to spare to pass clear of them. The best idea is to talk to the pilot and forget the rocks. This is one time you trust your pilot and your God.

CHAPTER TWENTY TWO

AT THE ENTRANCE TO all Russian ports there is an imaginary geographical boundary line, which you cross at your peril without permission. On arrival of the port of Murmansk at the pilot station I called port control for permission to enter until I was blue in the face. There seemed to be endless women chattering away on channel 16 the port control frequency. With the best use of international seafarers language. In no uncertain manner I eventually got through to port control and permission to enter. On passage up the river and passing Severomorsk the Russian Naval base, which sits on a bay just by the river, it had many interesting ships in port at that time. A few ships were lying in the river at the entrance to the bay. A most pathetic attempt was made by them to put up a smoke screen between the port and us. Our quartermaster on the wheel nearly caused the third world war. Whilst passing Severomorsk he put the wheel the wrong way in response to an order from the pilot. The pilot got himself into an awful mental state. Luckily the officer of the watch soon sorted out both quartermaster and the pilot.

On completion of tying up and getting the gangway out the usual crowd of shore officials made their way onboard, most of whom were women. The usual routine at a Russian port is for the captain to sign all the bills for the ship on arrival. It matters little when they are signed really because the Russians have already been put in funds by the owner before the arrival of the ship. The rate of exchange used for dealing with ships is usually one rouble to the pound sterling. I sat down to sign the bills for the young lady waiting for them. I noticed the bill for the captain's car this time was 100 roubles. The usual rate for the car is 9 roubles. I looked at the young lady and said "Mrs dear, there is no hope of me signing for a captains car. Certainly not at 100 roubles especially when it is for something one doesn't get to use."

She became very annoyed and said. "All captains sign for their car, you must sign." I told her in no uncertain terms I was not signing for the price they wanted from me, it is robbery. She then reminded me they, the port authorities were bringing a 'chamber orchestra' to play for the crew to night at the International Seamen's Club also a lady to give them a talk on 'Perestroika' I said, "My dear, I think my crew would prefer a dance band and some good looking young girls." At that she lifted her papers and stormed out of my cabin.

A couple of hours later a rather important looking lady and gentleman arrived onboard. The guy said "Captain why will you not sign for your car"

I said. "I don't want a car I don't want to go ashore."

He replied "you'll pay whether you use the car or not."

I was beginning to get annoyed "OK mister if that is the case, I want the car, now". This guy then said.

"Why do you want it, you cannot go any where. Where do you want to go to?"

By this time the steam was coming out of my ears. I looked him strait in the eyes and said. "If your going to deduct 100 roubles from the ships funds for a car I don't really want, then get it here now. I want to go to your famous war museum and I want to go to the gravesite of the British Merchant Navy from the Second World War". In the meantime the girl who accompanied him had come to take one of my younger seaman, a rather bolshie young lad, to the hospital. The young lad came up to my cabin to contact this young Russian courier. He looked at her, tickled her under her chin with his forefinger and said. "Come along princess."

I thought sure she was going to cry rape. She shouted at the young lad.

"I am no Princess, I am Natalia"

My car did arrive with the same guy driving. He sounded and later confirmed that he was a Director of Interflot. We arrived at the museum and at the door stood some people waiting for my arrival. I was certainly getting first class treatment. Having been shown into the director's office a young lady was sent for who spoke flawless English to act as my guide. For someone interested in the history of the Second World War it was a wonderful tour. The museum had been a hospital during the war. It must be remembered the German front line was only thirty miles away to the westward. They only had one small photograph of an allied merchant ship discharging her cargo of war supplies at Murmansk. That led to a great discussion in the director's office after the tour about the Second World War. I was the only visitor to the museum in the past year. It was seldom opened, it didn't attract much interest. The staff just couldn't believe that the Germans had bombed Belfast during the war. Actually they found it hard to believe that Northern Ireland was even in the war. I soon changed their ideas about the Second World War. They were very proud to tell me that the picture often seen in magazines and on war films about the fall of Berlin showing the Red flag being hoisted above the Reichstag in Berlin. The lad who actually hoisted the flag up was from Murmansk. When we came out of the museum it was too dark to go to the Allied Seaman's War Cemetery. My hosts then insisted on taking me to the International Seaman's Club where they very kindly piled me with books all in Russian and little gifts for my wife.

A couple of my crew had a nasty incident ashore

having walked out from their most boring lecture on Perestroika. Whilst walking up a street some one from behind caught one of my sailors by the arm from behind. The AB immediately turned round and hit the guy a punch on the jaw knocking him to the ground. By this time a lot of people gathered one of who was a uniformed policeman. The guy who received the very sore jaw was apparently a gentleman from the KGB. The uniformed policeman and some passers-by saw what had happened and told the KGB man he brought it on himself the way he approached a stranger in the town. I was delighted to learn that no charges would be brought against my sailor.

When sailing time came I was really pleased to get away. A couple of custom police or what they call border guards came onboard just before sailing. I asked the agent.

"What did these guys want are they going to search the ship."? I couldn't help but laugh when she said.

"No, no, captain we only search Polish and Romanian ships." I was handed a cable from the owners advising me not to use the leads on the way south. There is no great hurry for the ship therefore it is not worth the extra expense in pilotage fees to use the leads.

We left the berth on a clear crisp dark night. The air Temperature was very low as we proceeded to sea. After dropping the pilot our course was set for the

North Cape. There was the most wonderful display of Aurora Borealis to watch just as the watches were changing. The Chief Officer just took over his watch when the lookout reported a large ship with no lights four points on the starboard bow. The sea was so calm that the Aurora was reflected in it. The ship with no lights could be seen quite clearly dark against the lighter sea reflecting the sky. It was a large submarine. I said to the chief officer.

"It is really quite eerie up here on the top of the world, there is a funny feeling about the place."

"Yes I agree said the mate, something sinister about the place even more so with that submarine so close by."

The chief officer had his binoculars continuously trained on the sub.

"He is altering course coming, round our stern."

The mate reported. "Call him up and see if he answers, mate."

"Look captain she is starting to dive, there, she's away."

"OK, good night I'm off to my bunk. We should be passing the North Cape in about sixteen hours if this weather keeps up. See you in the morning, mate."

Late the following afternoon the radio officer handed me a weather report, which was rather ominous, a very deep depression of the Southwest of

England was giving very severe weather all along the coasts of the UK. It was something we had to try and avoid. I was very concerned because of the low stowage factor of the cargo (That meant although the ship was loaded to her marks the cargo did not fill the holds. There was a lot of free space in the holds because of that. It also meant in extreme conditions the cargo could move). I considered the best action to take was to heave too and let the storm pass ahead of us. I left instructions in my night order book to watch the wind very closely in order to ascertain the movement and direction of the storm. By breakfast time it was obvious the storm* had altered its course and was heading directly up the Norwegian coast towards us. The mate had all hands on deck getting the ship fully battened down. All the deadlights were screwed well down including the storm plates on the lower deck. Everything for'ard was checked and secured. We did not want a repetition of our call in the Firth of Fourth. At 1300 I was having a nap on my settee when my phone rang. I was wanted on the bridge. When I arrived on the bridge and saw the sea that was running I hardly needed to be told of the reason I was called to the bridge. Although the ship was pitching and rolling easily. The officer on watch had broken out in a most awful rash. As I stood beside the officer of the watch studying the weather. I could see the weather was most definitely getting worse. The seas were getting bigger and the ship was beginning to pitch more violently necessitating a further reduction in engine speed. The iron mike (That is the automatic steering gear) was beginning to work very hard to the extent I had the watches doubled up and the wheel put on (That is a man to steer the ship rather than be in automatic). All the time the sea seemed to becoming steeper with the bow lifting higher into the air. At that time the chief officer who was watch below came into the wheelhouse. I said to him, "What is wrong with you can't sleep"? He said in jest," The bloody mackerel are making faces at me through the port". I noticed out of the corner of my eye that the officer of the watch was continuously pulling up his shirt and examining himself. I took a look at him and discovered to my horror that the rash he had on his stomach at 1300 had now reached his shoulder blades on his back. It was spreading at an alarming rate. I sent him below to get himself sorted out. His watch was just about up anyway, The chief officer would be back on the bridge soon in any case.

I had now come to the conclusion that the sea was now becoming +dangerous. I rang the chief engineer and asked him to come to the bridge. As he came into the wheelhouse I said to him

"Chief the sea is now becoming dangerous and I'm going top have to use the engineer more in nursing her. She is continuously falling of the sea. I must keep her head into the sea, if she broaches too with this cargo it may shift causing untold danger if not worse. Take the UMS off and man the enginroom." "Captain what ever you wish, I think that is a splendid idea." At this time one of the AB's appeared on the bridge offering me a mug of cocoa. He looked me straight in the eye as he handed me the cocoa and said "OK, captain" I knew what this mug of cocoa was all about. He was looking at my face for signs of fear. He didn't see any but I knew within myself that come darkness. When I couldn't see the big seas approaching the ship I wouldn't be able to handle the ship, as I should. That is when I would be a very worried captain.

As the ships head lifted to a big sea her head always seemed to fall away to starboard, in which case I gave the engine a kick ahead with the wheel hard'a'port to help her climb the sea and keep on course without falling off to the sea. As she went over the top of the sea I would reduce speed to keep her from burying deep into the sea. This exercise was carried out all through the night. I knew if she broached the chances were very high that I would loose the ship and that we would all be lost. Nobody was going to be able to rescue us in this weather out here.

I couldn't understand Radio 'Bodo' which is a radio station on the Norwegian coast just south of us giving force 7 to 8 winds when we were experiencing full storm force winds. With literally mountainous seas. By this time we were just west of the Lofoten Islands the date October 1987. I sent Bodo a message to that effect. I also had sparkey send a TTT TTT TTT message, which is an urgent call to all ships. In it

I included a severe storm warning. (Some years later I met the captain of a Jebsen Line Bulkcarrier, which was astern of me about ten miles away although I did not know that at the time. She was bound for Caen from Spitsbergen with a cargo of coal. Her captain was also a very worried man about the weather conditions, because he was not experiencing the weather being broadcast by Bodo Radio. He was very pleased to have picked up my TTT message.)

To try and see the big seas approaching the ship as they broke across the deck I put the floodlights on. That was a very stupid thing to do because the light was reflected on the spray to such an extent that I was really blinded by the reflection. I put the floodlights out and just tried to get the feel the ship as she lifted to the sea. I was totally exhausted and very frightened. I knew there was a limit to what one can do in such weather one thing for sure you can't play God. I was really worried when sparkey reported he couldn't get my signals away because the aerials were all coated in salt He eventually transmitted them when the sun came up in the morning and the aerials dried off sufficient to allow radiation. By noon the next day there was a slight easing of the wind though the sea was still big and dangerous. We made steady progress towards the Elbe but only at nine knots. The Elbe Pilot cutter was off station because of the weather. She had positioned herself along way up the river nearer Brunsbuttle. The second pilot came onboard at Cruxhaven, which was rather out of the ordinary.

At that stage in the river we were still taking water on deck mostly heavy spray. The chief engineer came to see me. I was rather taken aback because he took my hand and said "Captain I just want you to know I will sail with you anytime anywhere" That was quite an accolade to a captain especially coming from a chief engineer. It was a very commendable gesture on his part and I took it as such.

After berthing and inspecting the cargo when we got the hatches opened. It looked as though we had cargo damage in No: 1 hatch and a little in No: 2 hatch. Ingress of water had taken place in those hatches in way of the joints of the hatch covers. Barges were brought alongside to receive the damaged cargo. Considering what we had come through the damage was little it amounted to just less than three hundred tons. There was no structural damage to the ship at all except of course crockery. It took us nearly four days to get the cargo discharged because the damaged cargo required man handling and the use of shovels. There wasn't much interest in going ashore not one man wanted a sub everyone just wanted to turn in and sleep.

The picture on the front cover was taken during the above storm in the Arctic Ocean.

CHAPTER TWENTY THREE

OUR NEXT ORDERS WERE to proceed to Rotterdam to load a full cargo of Bulk Aluminium for Strumavik in Iceland. What a trip in wintertime. Our sister ship was running all the time to South Africa which we would have liked to have done for a change, especially at this time of the year. In fact quite a few of our ships were on that run. At least we weren't given time to get bored on a along sea passage.

In eighteen hours we were entering Rotterdam to load in the Botleck from another ship. Actually a Chinese ship which had brought our cargo from Australia for transhipment at Rotterdam for Iceland. Whilst loading at Rotterdam a great effort was made to keep the cargo dry whilst transferring it from the Chinese ship. We all knew at Iceland that would be the least of their worries, whether the cargo was wet or dry on delivery. On passage to Iceland the weather west of the Pentland Firth was very bad with seventeen meter seas according the our weather forecasts. I phoned Bracknell weather centre direct to confirm the weather forecast. It was confirmed as bad as I had feared. Rather than risk unwarranted storm damage and put fuel up the funnel and get nowhere. I sheltered by putting the anchor down by Bass Island for two full days. A marine superintendent complained to me about the delay to the ship and further advised me that a much faster ship would get our berth causing further delay. What was I going to do? I suggested to him that next time he ensures that Jesus Christ was one of my crew and if I am good to him he might calm the sea for me. Or he might even give me a faster engine and then I would get to the berth before a ship which is already much faster than me.

When the storm abated sufficiently I was soon underway. Upon clearing the Pentland Firth the swell was still very big against which I made little headway. Under the circumstances the passage we made was quite good at just over nine knots. Our top economical speed was only 12.5 knots; we could do more at a very high expenditure of fuel. The faster ship had been and gone before we arrived. Whilst discharging the cargo and the ship gets higher and higher out of the water the discharging gear can't reach into the hold. Therefore it is necessary to put the ballast in whilst discharging the cargo. It is expected that the stevedore controlling the discharging gear manoeuvres it carefully. As we have very large ballast tanks running up the side of the ship to the main deck extreme care is required when sucking out the cargo. This guy thought he was in 'Barry's Dodgems.' He hit the ballast tanks on both side a heavy blow with his machine causing a severe rupture on each side of the ship. The out come of which was the ballast emptied into the hold causing flooding and considerable damage to the cargo. What happens next? The proverbial shit hits the fan. The big problem when such an accident happens is. At these discharging berths there is usually only one man controlling the discharging machine. When such an accident happens there is no labour available to clean up the mess in the holds. The crew although expected too, cannot do it either. Now is the time when the captain is expected to be God and work miracles with his crew. Each party endeavours to get the other to accept and sign for the damage. Needless to say each party refuses, the flash cars arrive down to the ship and the gentlemen in clean shirts and suits ascend the gangway wanting to either throw their weight around or weigh the captain up and down to see in their little minds if he can be bribed. I just look at them and tell them in a manner that leaves them in no doubt. They have damaged my ship leaving her in an unseaworthy state hence she cannot proceed to sea by law. I gave it to them in writing. It is a marvel what they can do when they have to.

Upon cleaning the holds and getting the repairs carried out we were watching the weather reports very closely and the agent very kindly collect the weather charts from the local meteorological offices each day. A very deep depression over the Saint Lawrence was deepening further and could cause us considerable trouble when we sail. Plotting the storm centre suggested that the storm should just be southwest of Iceland when we sail and eventually we would end up in the centre of it. I considered it best to let it pass ahead of us and then track round it as I made my way south. The problem with running from Iceland to Southern Ireland the weather is always on the beam. Where as crossing the Atlantic the weather is usually ahead. I waited for twenty-four hours before sailing to let the worse of the weather pass ahead. On sailing we tracked round the storm running with the sea on our starboard quarter. For the very first time when I was at sea my wife was so worried that she rang the office looking for news of my ship, dear bless her. I was very glad to get into the shelter of Loop Head and smooth water. The berth was ready for us at Aughinish so it was just a case of strait alongside and loaded. We loaded in twenty-two hours and away again to Rotterdam. The trip to Rotterdam was really lovely. The British Isles had a High Pressure area covering the whole country, which meant the air was cold and crisp with exceptional visibility.

Once again our discharging berth was in the Botleck, discharging taking place into barges. I often wondered how the families who live on the Dutch barges put up with the constant dust and dirt, which emanates from the cargo they are carrying. They live so close to it all and I suppose get few holidays to get away from it. The barges, which I have visited, were absolutely spic and span. One can't help wondering how they manage to keep them so clean in the environment in which they live and work.

There was a very good supply of barges which meant cargo would be discharged quickly no waiting for barges to arrive alongside. We had a pilot onboard and underway in twenty-four hours bound for Gdynia via the Kiel Canal. The passage down the Maas was good it seemed to be quite a quick trip to the pilot cutter. As the pilot was leaving and shaking hands with me he mumbled something about the visibility expected to be low to night in the North Sea. About an hour north of the Maas pilot station the visibility seemed to drop very quickly. In a very short space of time we were into dense fog. The watches were doubled up and the engine room advised of the possibility of a night of engine movements. There is always a lot of traffic about in this area. It is one of the busiest parts of the North Sea. I couldn't help thinking no sleep to night as I walked over to the radar. The officer of the watch had set up the secondary radar for plotting. Already he was calling out plotting information to me and my head just wasn't fully adjusted to receive it all. We were in the North East bound shipping lane bound up to the Texel Light and then up to the Elbe Light. Normally we would do this trip in about eighteen hours or less but in thick fog it will take much longer on reduced speed. Although the traffic in a shipping lane should all be going in the same direction. Fishing vessels are a law unto themselves and go back and forth as they please, especially so in this part of the world. Our speed by now had been reduced to about nine knots. The traffic showing on the radar was really dense. One good thing was I could hear the officer of the watch ring the stand-by man and order tea and toast. It is going to be a very long night on this bridge. Cocoa and toast or tea is going to be required to help us survive the night.

As we approached the Elbe Lt., Hamburg port control called us and asked that we should alter course fifteen degrees to starboard slowly so that they could identify us on their radar. When we considered it safe to do so we made the alteration as requested. Soon the pilot cutter could be identified on our radar working among the vessels picking up their pilots. Speed was reduced to slow ahead and when the cutter was 5 cables off we came down to dead slow ahead. The pilot was soon on the bridge and I was very pleased to see him. The Elbe Navigation or Port Control is first class. Like air traffic control with continuous advice coming from Port Control. We were bound for the Kiel Canal and Brunsbuttle. The pilot advised that the ice was thick at the entrance to the canal and bad in the canal but that the traffic in the canal had kept the Ice reasonably well broken. I had been standing by the radar since the previous morning and now I was beginning to feel the effects of it. The passage through the canal in these conditions would take at least twelve hours. A new pilot would board at Rendsburg for the remainder of the canal passage to Holtenau. After we cleared the locks at Holtenau we pushed ice through the bay to the Pilot station at Kiel were the ice was very thick. The pilot launch could not get alongside us because of the ice. The pilot had to walk across the ice to the pilot cutter; it was rather difficult for us to get underway because it was so thick. There seemed to be a fair amount of traffic about, all of it trying to force their way through the Ice. Normally we would do Kiel to Gydina in about twenty-five hours but under the present weather conditions it could take two or three days depending entirely on the ice. I would be happy if only the fog would disperse. It was the morning of the third day when we arrived of our loading berth as the fog was just beginning to clear.

The usual officials arrived onboard all looking for their tokens of appreciation as they often referred to what they could cadge. I made it clear to them that I had been on the bridge of my ship for four days and was very tired. I invited them to attend to their business as quickly as they could because I was going direct to bed. The chief officer would deal with any further business concerning the ship. They all disappeared complete with their 'goodies' with somewhat indecent haste. I went to my cabin and started to shake I seemed to be trembling all over and I couldn't think why. When I turned in, at first I couldn't sleep but I soon went out like a light falling into a very deep sleep. I continuously ask myself as do many other masters Why stay on the bridge when your so exhausted for the want of sleep that you couldn't make a quick and wise decision in an emergency anyway? We all know in the event of an accident with your ship the first question to be asked in a Marine Court

(Investigation) of Law. Where was the captain at the time of the accident? If he was not on the bridge, why not? The law expects masters to have the powers of God not just to be next to God.

That night I thought it would be nice to go up the road to somewhere pleasant and have a drink ashore. The chief and I went to one of the better-known hotels if not the best. As we entered the Foyer the chief remarked how well furnished the place was actually quite good overall. "Captain, there is a hell of a lot of women sitting about here."

"Ah, said I and really good looking as well".

As we sat down we ordered our usual Bicardi and Coke. When the drinks arrived they looked like trebles.

"Do you notice these girls are all staring at us captain"?

"Yes I do indeed chief they're all on the game, that is why. They all love a baldy guy you know, that is why they keep looking over at us, it's that bald batch of yours is the attraction." "Actually I don't like being stared at like that, captain."

I suggested to him that was we should take a walk up into the town to somewhere different. "Chief a few more drinks like that and you just never know where you'll end up."

"Yes, I think your right captain, Actually those three drinks were enough for me to-night, I'm quite happy to go back to the ship if you like."

"OK chief lets go."

Due to the general weather conditions loading was rather slow. The weather just became colder and the weather reports which we received form Stockholm concerning ice in the Baltic were not very encouraging. Because of our draft we were going to have to use the Belts leaving the Baltic for the North Sea. When there is no rush for the cargo there is no point paying canal dues to use the Kiel Canal. Eventually the cargo was loaded but there seemed to be a lot of rubbish in it like bits of metal lumps of wood, which was liable to cause damage to the discharging belts at West Thurrock on the Thames. The receivers were warned by cable of the state of the cargo.

The pilot left by tug not because we needed a tug but because the pilot boat could not get alongside because of the heavy ice. Once clear of the breakwaters it was a case of pushing hard all the way against the ice. The noise of the ice scrapping along the ships side was deafening. On arrival at the entrance to Fehmarn Belt the ice was so thick that I had my doubts about getting through it. With great effort and maybe a lot of 'Gaelic' we pushed our way up through the Great Belt to the Kattegat. The ice by the Skaw had melted considerably as we approached deeper water and with the melting ice we increased our speed. Thank God the Thames does not freeze up like the Baltic though having said that some years the Baltic is clear of ice

Extensive Brash Ice in the Baltic

except perhaps the head of the Gulf of Bothnia.

Upon arrival at West Thurrock the Senior Marine Superintendent arrived onboard. The manner in which he greeted me led me to think he had something on his mind. He looked at me and said. "Ralph the company would like you to study for the Thames pilots licence. It would mean a lot more money in your pocket and your pension. What do you think?"

"Captain let me think about it?" "I know it would also bore the pants off me to the extent that money would not pay one to trade up and down the East Coast all their life."

"I can promise you, you would not be kept on that run all the time. Only when your ship would be on a CEGB charter. I know you lost a lot of pension when you were ashore this would give you a chance to recoup it."

"OK, I'll do it on that promise but I could not spend my life on the East Coast."

"That's a promise just if your ship comes onto a CEGB charter. Anyway your next orders are a big NATO exercise so that will give you something to think about."

The lad from our London office came onboard to see me about the exercise and advise me all about it. "Due to the problem with filters needing cleaning so often because of slow steaming in convoy an extra engineer would join also an extra officer to assist with the amount of bridge work running in a convoy. I understand you will be commodore ship but that is to be confirmed. You will have two naval Lieutenant Commanders and one Lieutenant also six ratings for communication work. You will also get an extra steward because of the extra workload in the saloon. All your sailing instructions are in that big envelope to be opened when dropping outward pilot." We continued our conversation over a cup of tea on the pros and cons of studying for a Thames pilot's licence. I advised him that all things being equal we should get away tomorrow evening. When we disembark the outward pilot at that point we would come under charter to the Ministry of Defence for the duration of the exercise.

Upon arrival at the convoy assembly point I was given an anchorage position and asked to fly our signal letters. The Royal Naval personnel assigned to our ship would join in the morning. The picket launch, which would bring the naval contingent to us, would also take my radio officer and my self to the convoy conference. We were told we should wear our civilian dress not uniform. That order annoyed me intensely it smacked of the orders given to masters during the 1914-18 war. During the First World War when ships captains had to visit Royal Naval guard ships for instructions they were required to wear their civilian gear. That was the time when there was considerable friction between the Royal Navy and the Merchant Service, as it was known then over uniforms. The

Merchant Service was just beginning to wear their new uniforms and the Royal Navy did not like it one little bit.

I was just as proud of my uniform as the Royal Navy was of theirs. I'm dammed if I was going to let them tell me when I can wear my uniform. I had declined to visit the Royal Navy before on their Thursday war (At that time the navy exercised their ships in the channel on a Thursday. They sometimes took visitors to sea with them to watch their ships at work.) In the channel over the same rule and I certainly hadn't changed my attitude to it. Just as I received my instructions my chief officer came to see to ask if he could accompany me to the convoy conference. He was a commissioned commander with the Royal Naval Reserve. I instructed him and sparks to be at the gangway in full uniform at 1000 to come with me to the convoy conference. If they didn't have a decent uniform for whatever reason they couldn't come with me I would go alone. The second officer would attend to our visitors by signing them on and instructing them on our ships safety drill.

The conference was held in a large drill hall of the local naval reserve. Everyone present was dressed in uniform with the exception of one individual who was wearing a brace and bib dungarees a pair of clogs and a Breton steaming bonnet (a French fisherman's blue cap). By his dress I assumed him to be a master of a German snake ('Snake' is the name given to a type of long low air drafted ship capable of steaming far up the long continental rivers from the sea.). A Royal Navy petty officer addressed us all requesting that we all stand up when the commanding officer of the exercise entered the room. The commanding officer was a German Admiral. My first thoughts were how young he looked; he didn't look any older than my third officer. Different naval officers addressed us continuously using acronyms. They used so many acronyms in their address that I thought they were using a different language maybe Irish.

Picket boats manned by wrens were at the quay waiting to take us back to our ships. We also had a television crew with us for the voyage. The convoy put to sea as per our sailing instructions. Each ship took up its assigned position in the convoy. Our two naval Lt.commanders advised me that they would be available at any time if required. "Yes, indeed you will, I want one of you on the bridge at all times. Which means keeping a watch and working watch and watch on the bridge. I suggest you work a dogwatch but I will leave that up to you. You will not be required to work a meal relieve. You must remember however, that the senior officer of the watch will be the ships officer. I want you to sign my standing orders and ensure you always read and initial my night orders. Is that all understood gentlemen?"

"Very good sir, thank you."

The first escort was German. During the night

Naval Exercises in North Atlantic

there was a problem with this escort because my second officer took our ship out of the convoy and when he considered we were in a safe position called me to the bridge. Eventually we all resumed our designated positions. Once we were in international waters we got down to real business and opened the bond giving everyone a bond issue. Our Royal Naval contingent never expected this and such a variety as well. I was never quite sure how information passed around a convoy but next day a helicopter landed on our deck enquiring if they could participate in the bond issue. I think these guys thought we had a TESCO off licence with us. After this exercise we still had our normal commercial voyage to do. It was important to get the television interview over and done with. We wanted to fly the television crew back to the UK so that they could get their programme broadcast as soon as possible on the news network.

Upon the completion of the exercise after twelve days. Sparks, the chief officer and myself together with the masters and the officers of the other ships in the convoy were taken ashore to a large military barracks for a convoy postmortem. Again in their address to the convoy officers. I felt there was a totally unnecessary excessive use of acronyms by the Royal Navy officers and I told them so. I further told them.

"That it was bordering on downright rudeness using acronyms to the extent they did when they knew the officers from the Merchant Ships have no idea what they mean. In so far as the exercise in general. It may have been of great assistance to the Royal Navy but as far as we are concerned it was a waste of time. The Merchant Navy learned nothing. I would have thought the Royal and Merchant Navy would have worked as a team for the common good of the convoy. As far as I could observe the old adage of. 'We're the sheep dogs you're the sheep' is ingrained in the Royal Navy to the extent that it sours the relationship between the two services. As a boy my elders always told me that at sea and I think it still stands to day, unfortunately. I think the Royal Navy has a lot to learn from the Scandinavian navies."

After I had made my statement and the conference ended many officers of various nationalities came over and shook my hand saying. A Danish officer said "Captain I couldn't miss that voice anywhere. Remember me, we exercised together before in the Baltic"? As he extended his arm to shake my hand he said.

"What you just said captain is so true and it is time it was said."

A great many NATO officers agreed with my remarks. Except the Americans they just glared at me and said nothing. A Royal Naval commander tried to address me in a phoney Northern Ireland accent with a phoney Paisley like dialect. Needless to say he got short shift and which is best not repeated.

CHAPTER TWENTY FOUR

Whilst on leave I talked to many of my seafaring friends with a view to forming an organisation for the benefit of retired members. There was an awful spate of redundancies in the Merchant Navy at that time. Leaving many men on the beach at a loose end. The armed forces all had their ex-service organisations to help them settle outside the services when they were discharged, we had nothing. Through organisations like of the Royal British Legion the armed services also reaped many accolades for their war service. Seafarers had nothing and I had made up my mind to do something about that. Many of the seamen returning from the Falklands war felt that the nation never had any interest in the Merchant Navy. Much to the total shame of the British nation. Merchant seamen were never allowed to take part in the Remembrance Day parade past the cenotaph in Whitehall until 2002. They had been ignored for nearly eighty years by a nation whose very lifeline was its Merchant Navy.

I had been elected a councillor of N.U.M.A.S.T. some years ago, which gave me an insight to a part of the Merchant Navy somewhat unknown to many of its members. All during that time I had heard so many seamen complain about the total lack of recognition of the Merchant Navy. I decided I would rectify that someway or other. There is so much about the Merchant Navy that even the members know little about. Particularly Mariners Park at Wallasey and the work of the Merchant Navy Welfare Board. Not forgetting the sterling work carried out by NUMAST (National, Union, of Marine Aviation & Shipping Transport Officers)serving on many international committees.

During the year 1992 I had been in and out of hospital in Norway and Iceland and many days at a time at home in local hospitals suffering from severe attacks of renal colic the pain from which I have been assured by ladies to be worse than childbirth. The time came when I had to do my Merchant Navy medical examination. The doctor gave me a thorough examination and politely failed me. Just a few days after that I was standing talking to my wife as she made the breakfast when I felt a funny feeling in my arms. I collapsed onto the floor, my wife immediately called a doctor and the 'heart ambulance.' Within minutes I was in the intensive care ward of our local hospital, I had had a heart attack. I spent a few days in intensive care and a few days in an ordinary ward. The day I was discharged from hospital and arrived home. That night I took the worst attack of renal colic I ever had, an ambulance was called about two in the morning when I was rushed to hospital again for another stay.

One fact was definite without any shadow of a doubt my seagoing days were finished. As I looked around Northern Ireland I noticed the complete lack of any thought whatsoever for its seamen compared to England. Yet, there were large seafaring communities throughout the Province. In order to overcome this shortcoming I put an advertisement in the Belfast Telegraph calling all merchant seamen to attend a meeting in a local hotel in Carrickfergus. The support at the meeting to form a Merchant Navy Association was very in encouraging. A committee was formed and everyone present paid a subscription of ten pounds. Arrangements were made to hold a meeting each month in the present hotel. I agreed or at least my good wife did, allowed the spare room in my home to be turned into an office for the benefit of the association. The Royal Naval Association was advised of the formation of the new Merchant Navy Association in the Province. They in turn welcomed us and did much to help make our association a success by participating in many of the events we organised. During the past twelve years there has been considerable rapport and co-operation between the two associations.

I was elected chairman of the MNA (Merchant Navy Association). One thing which was agreed in committee, if the Merchant Navy was going to gain recognition by the populace as a whole it would have to bring its very existence to the attention of the nation. It would have to copy the other ex-service associations in how they presented themselves. They would have to march in public and have their own standards. It would be imperative that they drew attention to themselves. I thought they would find such behaviour a total anathema. They moaned and groaned a lot but I forgot practically all were members of some form of lodge part of the very nature of the male population in the Province. Everyone in the Province loves a church parade. The other ex-service men have their special days and accompanying church parade. So we had to have ours. It was necessary to adapt a church, which was welcoming to all religions. The Parish Church of Saint George's made us most welcome and has remained our adapted church to this day notwithstanding the fact that every member has his own church.

The Royal Air Force Association had its 'Battle of Britain' day, the Army its 'Battle of the Somme' day in Northern Ireland and of course the Royal Naval Association its 'Battle of Trafalgar' day the Merchant navy Association decided it would have it's 'Battle of the Atlantic' day to be held on a suitable Sunday in May. The month of May was chosen because it was the month of May when the allies started to defeat the U-Boats. I had never organised a parade before but my memory of my days in the sea cadets came to the fore. On our first parade we paraded our new standard, which carried the names of all the famous convoys the Merchant Navy participated in. The Royal Naval Association turned out in support of us. The parade was a great success. I had organised with the help of the RAF for a Catalina Flying Boat to pass over the parade in the same direction. As it marched down High Street. The RAF flight controller was the on the top of the large government building in High Street directing the aircraft. After the parade the Royal Naval Association put their club at our disposal in order that we might have a reception there after the parade.

The association had no means of support save for the member's subscriptions, which at that time was about ten pounds annually. The question was how do we get money. I suggested we have a concert in the city not forgetting I had never run a concert in my life, I did however run a kiddies fancy dress parade on a passenger ship once. I agreed to cover the losses personally if the concert was a failure. The concert was a huge success but a very big undertaking for one person. Each year after that we had our annual concert under the banner of a *"Nautical Fantasia."* Every concert was a success financing the association for ten years. I was left to organise the concert myself every year and when the officers of the association including the most senior failed to lend their total support it was time for me to stop, so that was the end of the concerts.

I approached the admiralty with a view to having one of the North of Ireland flotilla facilitate a wreath laying ceremony at sea in commemoration of the Battle of the Atlantic. I made my request to Flag Officer Scotland and Northern Ireland. My request was granted and so we went to sea on the Saturday before our Remembrance service for the 'Battle of the Atlantic' each year. I and six members of the MNA together with six members of the RNA made up the wreath laying party each year. A wreath was also laid on behalf of the Maritime Institute of Ireland in remembrance of those from Southern Ireland who lost their lives in the Battle of the Atlantic. For ten years the Royal Navy facilitated our wreath laying in the Irish Sea for which we will be forever in their debt. The apogee of the Merchant Navy Association was when the Belfast City Council through the good offices of the association conferred the Freedom of the City of Belfast on the Merchant Navy.

In time the association became a registered charity in Northern Ireland, which enabled it to become a constituent member of the Merchant Navy Welfare Board. A considerable amount of welfare work was attempted through the good offices of a lady who after a course of training by the Merchant Navy Welfare Board became a voluntary welfare worker for the association. The association was going from strength to strength.

The first Battle of the Atlantic parade was made into a video and after twelve years I watched it one evening. It was really sad to do so, many of the members who had taken part in that parade had all past west (A nautical euphemism for died). Others had fallen into ill health and unable to attend meetings, many could no longer drive at night. Like all elderly people memory was becoming rather short and general interest in the association was beginning to leave much to be desired. Unfortunately with the considerable reduction of the Merchant Navy there are no new members coming forward. The lack of new members seems to be common to all ex-service associations. How long the association will continue is a matter for conjecture. Certainly its activities are only a shadow of its former self. My own medical problems were such that my family both nuclear and extended implored me to resign. As I could do well without the worries of the Merchant Navy Association I took their advice. I resigned.

This year, 2005, has been declared nationally as 'The Year of the Sea.' To bring to public attention the exploits of the Merchant Navy in Peace and War. I had great pleasure – indeed honour- to arrange, with the support of my colleagues, an exhibition onboard the First World War cruiser HMS Caroline, moored here in Belfast. The exhibition depicting the history of the Merchant Navy since 1922 when, by Royal decree, the then Merchant Service was henceforth known as the Merchant Navy.

I have had nearly sixty years participating in various facets of the maritime industry and at the end of it all I have had no regrets.

ISBN 1-41205558-X

Printed in Great Britain
by Amazon